THE
San Juan
MOUNTAINS

THE SanJuan MOUNTAINS

A CLIMBING & HIKING GUIDE

ROBERT F. ROSEBROUGH

CORDILLERA PRESS, INC.

Publishers in the Rockies

Library of Congress Cataloging-in-Publication Data

Rosebrough, Robert F.
  The San Juan Mountains.

  Bibliography: p.
  Includes index.
  1. Mountaineering—San Juan Mountains (Colo. and
N.M.)—Guide-books. 2. Hiking—San Juan Mountains
(Colorado. and N.M.)—Guide-books. 3. San Juan Mountains
(Colo. and N.M.)—Description and travel—Guide-books.
I. Title.
GV199.42.S26R67   1986   917.88'38   86-4530
ISBN: 0-917895-07-X

Printed in the United States of America

ISBN: 0-917895-07-X

First Edition
1 2 3 4 5 6 7 8 9

Cover photographs by Spencer Swanger.

Maps courtesy of Ada Rosebrough.

To my father, Haskell, who introduced me to the mountains and to my daughter, Mary Ellen, with the hope that she will have an opportunity to share the experience.

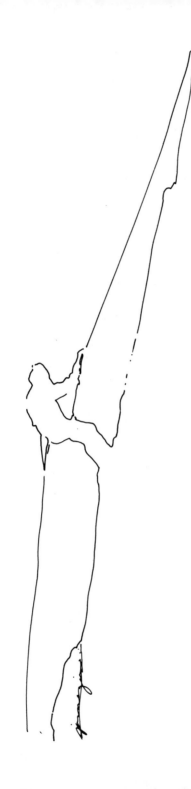

Contents

Preface

On the whole, the San Juans are sparsely traveled and infrequently climbed. As in other parts of Colorado, the crowds tend to congregate on a few popular trails and on the standard approaches and routes to the fourteeners. During the summer preceding the publication of this guide, I climbed over fifty thirteeners in the San Juans. Only twice, on Mount Emma and Peak Three of all places, did I run into other climbing parties.

Undoubtedly, part of the reason that the San Juans are not overcrowded in most areas is that there are no large metropolitan areas close by. Another reason is that there is an almost overwhelming variety of peaks and trails available. Thirteen of Colorado's fifty-four fourteeners and twenty-nine of Colorado's one hundred highest peaks are located in the San Juans. There are hundreds of peaks over thirteen thousand feet in elevation. The San Juans offer not only a lot of peaks to climb, but also many different types of climbs. There is something for everyone, from walkups, like San Luis and Redcloud, to severe technical climbs like the east face of Monitor Peak and the, as yet unclimbed, east face of Pigeon Peak.

If it accomplishes nothing else, I would hope that this guide would let the hikers and climbers in the San Juans know they have alternatives to such overcrowded areas as Chicago Basin and Yankee Boy Basin. In the vast majority of areas in the San Juans, hikers and climbers can still find the solitude and serenity which we seek in our wilderness ventures.

This guide is not, and does not claim to be, complete. It is, however, representative of the major areas in the San Juans. Although you are given a lot to choose from, do not let this guide limit your ambitions. There are certainly other worthwhile and challenging peaks, trails, and climbing routes which you will not find within the pages of this book.

I hope that this guide will give you an idea of where the trails and peaks are, how to get there, and a general idea of what you will encounter along the way. If you are looking for a detailed "blow by blow" account of what to expect, however, you will need to look elsewhere. No guide, this one included, will allow you to climb something you were not otherwise able to climb. *A guide cannot be a substitute for mountaineering judgment.*

The essence of mountaineering is calculating and applying your abilities in the mountain setting. Inevitably, you must make decisions based on a variety of factors such as your own capabilities, the weather, the time of day, and the seasons, which this guide has no control over. The bottom line is that you must gain and then apply sound mountaineering judgment.

I would hope that this guide will allow you to pick out new objectives and give you a general idea of what to expect. At that point, I would suggest leaving the guide behind. Once you leave your vehicle, let your actions be determined by your own abilities and judgments rather than the pages of this book.

As this guide and other publications make the trails and peaks of the San Juans more accessible, hikers and climbers need to keep in mind that they bear a heavy responsibility to preserve the wilderness for future usage. It is essential not only for ourselves, but future generations, that we both preach and practice an ethic which minimizes our impact on the wilderness which we enjoy so much.

Acknowledgments

There may be a day when I can say that I've climbed everything there is to climb in the San Juans. At present, however, that remains a goal rather than a reality. In order to make this guide as comprehensive as possible, it has been necessary for me to rely on previously published route descriptions in mountaineering journals and climbing magazines. In addition, I solicited reports from climbers active in the area. The source of the route description is included in the text. When no source is mentioned, you can blame me.

With regard to publications, the Colorado Mountain Club's *Trail and Timberline (T&T)* is the leading source of published route descriptions for the San Juans. I was also able to pick up a description or two of other routes, primarily technical, from *The American Alpine Journal (A.A.J.)*, *Climbing*, *The Chicago Mountaineer*, and *Summit*. Published reports tend to be a hit or miss affair. Some are detailed and accurate, while others are not. Whenever possible, I would suggest consulting the original text of any publications quoted. Frequently, space limitations prevented me from quoting the full text of an article or report.

For a couple of reasons, I feel that as a general rule route descriptions submitted by other climbers tend to be more reliable than published reports. First, I was able to solicit specific information. Second, I am confident that the climbers who contributed to this guide know what they are talking about. Each contributor is a knowledgeable climber who has been active in the San Juans. Among those who contributed information on routes and access are: Tim Duffy, Rich Riefenberg, Art Tauchen, Michael Covington, Jon Lawyer, Haskell Rosebrough, Ernie Stromeyer, Mike Butyn, Larry Coats, Tom Norton, Bill Henry, Jim Gehres, Kenneth Heil, Cy Dixon, Hal Brown, George Bell, George Bell, Jr., Bob Beverly, and Kent Beverly.

While researching the history of climbing in the San Juans, I was particularly pleased with the assistance given to me by a large group of climbers and historians. In particular, I would like to thank: Joe Kramarsic, Bill Bueler, Mike Foster, Robert M.

Ormes, John Nelson, Joe Stettner, Jack Fralick, R.J. Campbell, Bob Bliss, George Pokorny, Dick Guadagno, Paul Mahoney, Henry Buchtel, David Belknap, Earle R. Whipple, Sally Ross, David Carter, and John Filsinger.

A large part of any climbing history or guide are the photographs which bring the people, mountains, and routes to life. Again, a large number of people contributed, including: Mel Griffiths, Tom Sawyer, Tim Duffy, Ernie Stromeyer, Joe Merhar, Bob Beverly, David Kozak, Melinda Marinaro, George Bell, Werner Schnackenberg, Joe Stettner, Pat Armstrong, Bob Bliss, R.J. Campbell, Michael Covington, John Nelson, Louise Roloff, Antoine Savelli, Haskell Rosebrough, David Cooper, Carl Blaurock, Bill Bueler, Walt Borneman, Spencer Swanger, Stuart Krebs, John Filsinger, Doug Ward, and Jay Mason.

I would also like to thank Ada Rosebrough for her excellent work on the graphics and illustrations, James B. Joe for his illustration of the climber rappeling, and Fannie Azua for her patience while struggling to make sense of my illegible scribblings.

Climbing is always more enjoyable when shared with good friends. While good climbing partners are sometimes hard to come by, I have been blessed with three of the best in Ernie Stromeyer, Ike Weaver, and David Nordstrom. For fear of offending those who I would inevitably overlook in a list, I would also mention that I have enjoyed the company of a great many others on my climbs in the San Juans.

A supportive spouse is almost as hard to come by as good climbing partners. I have been doubly blessed. I owe much to my wife, Beth, for her support and patience.

As I close these acknowledgments, I am struck by two thoughts. First, I am somewhat taken aback by the help which I have received from so many people. In many respects, it has been a group effort. Second, in spite of this outpouring of assistance, more remains to be done. There are more peaks and routes worthy of description. There is more historical information waiting to be uncovered. There are many old slides and photographs stored away in dusty files waiting to be rediscovered. If you have criticisms, suggestions, photographs, or information which you would like to share with me, please do so. I can be reached by writing to 101 West Aztec, Suite B, Gallup, New Mexico 87301. I hope that the first edition of this guide will serve as a stepping stone toward a truly complete guide and history of the San Juans.

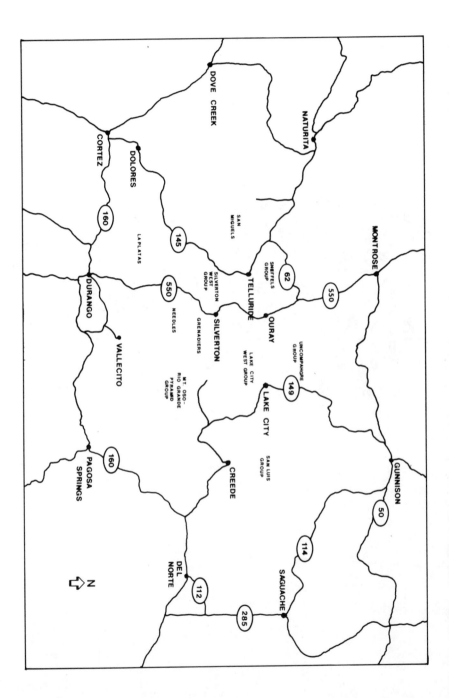

BEFORE YOU GO—
A Few Words of Advice

The mountains can be an unforgiving place for the inexperienced and ill-equipped. Lightning, avalanches, altitude sickness, hypothermia, rockfall, and many other hazards await the unsuspecting and unprepared. While this guide cannot begin to cover basic mountaineering subjects in depth, this chapter seeks to provide some basic hints and cautions. For the beginner, an excellent text on mountain hazards and the dos and don'ts of mountaineering in general is *Mountaineering: Freedom of the Hills*, published by The Mountaineers, 715 Pike Street, Seattle, Washington 98101.

If you lack experience in the mountains, the best way to gain it is to hike or climb with someone who has it. If you don't have a friend or relative who is willing to share his experience with you, one alternative is to join an organization such as the Colorado Mountain Club. Two of the Colorado Mountain Club groups climb primarily in the San Juans: the San Juan group whose members are located primarily in Durango, and the Western Slope group whose members are primarily in the Grand Junction-Montrose area. The officers of these groups change on a yearly basis, so if you are interested in joining, your best bet would be to contact the Colorado Mountain Club's main office at 2530 West Alameda Avenue, Denver, Colorado 80219 (phone number [303] 922-8315). The Colorado Mountain Club puts out both a summer and winter schedule of trips and climbs led by experienced climbers.

CLOTHING — The best method of dressing for the mountains is "layering." The principle behind layering is that the hiker or climber is better able to adjust his clothing needs by either stripping or adding additional layers of clothing as needed. This is particularly true in the San Juans where the southerly latitude and high altitude combine to create a wide range of temperatures and weather conditions.

There are three basic layers. The first layer of undergarments provides warmth and should also "wick" moisture away from the body. Medium- or light-weight polypropylene underwear works well. The second layer of insulating clothing can be comprised of a wide variety of materials. Bunting, pile, wool, and quilted polypropylene are all excellent insulators. If at all possible, cotton should be avoided since it loses its ability to retain body heat when wet. The third or outer layer is called the shell and should be comprised of waterproof materials. Currently a great debate rages over the effectiveness of synthetic shells which purport to be both waterproof and breathable. I have yet to find a shell which truly accomplishes both goals. My preference is to value waterproofing over breathability. To a certain extent, the benefits of breathable materials can be achieved by purchasing waterproof shells which are ventilated. Be wary of "water-resistant" materials. They simply don't do the job.

Outdoor wear should be comfortable and loose fitting. Fashion should be the last thing on your mind. In addition to the clothing which comprises the three layers discussed above, a good pair of gloves and a wool hat are necessities in the mountains. Many climbers also like to use gaiters, particularly when climbing in areas with loose scree, to prevent loose rocks from digging their way down into their boots. Gaiters are a necessity for winter and spring climbing.

FOOTWEAR — The current trend is toward lightweight footwear. Some hiking boots come close to actually being running shoes. Although very comfortable, the lightweight mountain hiking boots are not waterproof and are not effective when climbing snow or ice. All-leather boots can be waterproofed but are heavier. If I could wear only one pair of boots in the mountains, I would choose the lightest pair of all-leather boots that can be effectively waterproofed. In addition to all-around climbing boots, there are several specialized types of climbing shoes. Friction boots are essential for severe technical climbs. Heavy, inflexible plastic boots come in handy when climbing waterfall ice and alpine gullies. If you use friction boots or plastic boots, you will probably want a second pair of shoes to use for the approach.

ACCESSORIES — The first accessory that any climber or day hiker should consider purchasing is a medium-size day pack. Without a good day pack, you are extremely limited in what you can do. For climbers, one feature that you should look for is an ice ax loop. As for what you should put in a day pack, I recommend sunglasses, sun screen, insect repellent, tape or mole skin, a small first aid kit, toilet paper, water bottle, topo map, matches, small flashlight or headlamp, and a lunch.

CLIMBING EQUIPMENT — A thorough discussion of climbing equipment is beyond the scope of this guide. It is possible, however, to point out a few of the items which you should consider acquiring once you have grown tired of "walkups" and have begun progressing toward more difficult climbs. Probably the first item of climbing equipment you should consider purchasing is an ice ax. It is inevitable that you will encounter snow eventually. An ice ax will allow you to climb snowbanks with safety and will also facilitate glissade descents. Another early purchase should be a headlamp which will allow you to begin making alpine starts. I also find a headlamp to be more convenient around a camp than a flashlight.

If you are interested in winter or spring climbing or climbing alpine gullies, crampons are essential. Fifth class climbing will require a rope, carabiners, slings, and a variety of protection such as chocks, pitons, and friends. In purchasing a rope, you should consider either acquiring one eleven-millimeter rope either 150 or 165 feet in length or two nine-millimeter ropes which can be used in tandem. A "dry" rope is worth the extra expense. If you plan to use pitons as protection, an alpine hammer with curved pick is essential. Another item of climbing equipment which is essential for the San Juans is a good hard hat. If you climb long enough in the San Juans, sooner or later a rock will come whizzing past your head.

HIKING AND CLIMBING ETHICS — The style which most climbers seek to achieve is "clean climbing." This involves the use of protection which does not damage or alter the rock. If at all possible, climbers should use chocks or friends which can be removed without leaving a trace. Pitons inevitably leave a scar. Although some feel that pitons are "unethical," I feel that there is still a place for them in the San Juans. Most technical routes in the mountains (as opposed to crag climbing in areas such as Cracked Canyon or The Watch Crystal) are infrequently climbed and, hence, there is not as large a problem with defacing the rock. The use of a knifeblade or thin pitons is more easily justified since thin cracks are harder to protect with chocks or friends. Bolts should be avoided, if at all possible.

Hikers also should seek to minimize their impact on the environment. Several general rules apply. First, you should pack out everything that you have packed in. Second, always bury your waste and toilet paper. Third, do not cut or damage live vegetation. Fourth, use as small a fire as possible, and if there are existing pits, use them rather than building new ones. Fifth, don't cut switchbacks on trails, and sixth, do not roll rocks from the summits of peaks. Rolling rocks will damage your fellow climbers as well as the environment.

BACKPACKING — Entire books have been devoted to teaching all the dos and don'ts of backpacking. If you haven't been backpacking, ask an experienced backpacker to go over an equipment list with you before setting out. The essentials are a pack, sleeping bag, sleeping pad, ground cloth, food, small cookstove, utensils, flashlight, matches, water bottle, and a tarp or tent. Your goal should be to go as light as possible. Cut out as many of the frills as you can.

SEASONS — January, February, and March are the most difficult and dangerous months for climbing. Heavy snow cover and winter conditions are inevitable. All approaches must be accomplished either by snowshoes or skis. Although the cold and long approaches make climbing difficult, the real problem with climbing during these months is avalanches. Special care should be taken during, or immediately after, storms. During April and May you are sure to encounter a heavy snowpack but the snow is generally more stable. Snowshoes and skis are still required for approaches.

June is an unpredictable month in the San Juans. The depth of the snowpack from the preceding winter will dictate whether normal hiking and climbing will be possible in the early part of June. Many years there is still a snowpack down to the ten or eleven thousand-foot elevations in early June. By July the snowpack is generally gone except for the north slopes. During July, the flies and mosquitoes come out and the afternoon thunderstorms begin. The thunderstorms continue through August, as does the reduction of the snowpack which at this point is usually limited to the steep north faces and alpine gullies. July and August are always the most crowded months of the year.

September is my favorite month for climbing. The thunderstorms usually go away with cooler weather, as do the crowds and insects. Climbing conditions during October vary widely from year to year. You can expect a snowstorm sometime in October and, hence, you should be prepared to walk out through a foot or so of snow. November and December are always cold but they offer the best winter climbing conditions. The lower snow cover allows you to enjoy winter climbing without as much fear of avalanches.

GEOLOGY — The San Juans are largely composed of volcanic rock from the Tertiary period. Beginning about 40 million years ago, volcanos erupted violently, pouring incredible amounts of ash and lava over the region. In places, deposits built up to depths of 10,000 feet. Actual relief, however, was more like 3,000 or 4,000 feet because of the downward settling of the overburden.

The widespread volcanic activity continued for several million years and was centered primarily in the area north and east of the Needle Mountains. The repeated eruptions emptied the magma chambers under the base of volcanos, causing them to collapse, thereby forming circular basins bounded by arcuate faults called calderas. At present, fifteen such calderas have been identified in the San Juans. The intense volcanic era left several classes of volcanic rock, including lava flows formed from liquid magma, tuff formed from ash, and cinder pellets and breccia made of lava fragments.

The Needles and Grenadiers, which were called the "Quartzites" by the early surveyors, show no evidence of this volcanic era. Although they undoubtedly received some volcanic spillage from the eruptions, it has now been eroded away. The Needles consist of Precambrian granite and gneiss, while the Grenadiers, to the north, are made up of steeply dipping layers of Precambrian quartzite and slate. The West Needle Mountains are Precambrian metamorphic rock, mostly gneiss. The Animas River, which separates the Needles and West Needles, cuts down through the gneiss into still older metamorphic rock. Continuing west, the highest peaks consist primarily of uplifted and faulted Paleozoic sedimentary layers.

On the western fringe of the San Juans, both the La Platas and the San Miguels consist of several small masses of Tertiary igneous rock which have intruded into Paleozoic conglomerates, shales, and limestones.

Most of the mineralization in the San Juans has taken place near the igneous intrusions or around the rims of the calderas. This mineralization took place primarily during the Late Tertiary period. The search for minerals has been primarily centered in the areas near Ouray, Silverton, Telluride, Rico, and the La Platas. The Silverton caldera alone has produced more than $150 million in metals, primarily silver and gold.

The fire and volcanoes of the Tertiary period were followed by the ice and glaciation of the Quaternary period. The glacial era left us with beautiful, U-shaped valleys, cirques, and matterhorn-shaped peaks such as Wetterhorn, Golden Horn, and Pigeon.

MAPS — This guide should be used as a supplement to, rather than a replacement for, United States Geological Survey maps and Forest Service maps. In fact, in some instances the route descriptions given are useless unless read in conjunction with a topographic map. All but a few of the quad maps for the San Juans are 7.5 minute series rather than 15 minute series. USGS maps can be purchased from many sporting goods and mountaineering shops in the area or ordered directly from the USGS, Western Distribution Branch, Box 25286, Federal Center, Denver, Colorado 80225.

Forest Service maps are not of much use for locating climbing routes, but they are the best method of plotting out your approach by road. The Forest Service maps cover much larger areas than the quad maps and their road information is generally more current.

The San Juan, Rio Grande, Uncompahgre, and Gunnison national forests all cover portions of the San Juans. Forest Service maps can be ordered from Visitor Map Sales, USDA Forest Service, P.O. Box 25127, Lakewood, Colorado 80225.

A couple of suggestions are in order at this point, which might be helpful in sorting out the information in this guide. The mileages given for road access are based primarily on odometer readings and it is anticipated that in following the descriptions, you will measure mileage based on the odometer readings in your vehicle. Please keep in mind that odometer readings invariably differ from vehicle to vehicle and that you should, therefore, use the access descriptions in conjunction with the Forest Service map which applies to the area.

There are still an unusually large number of unnamed peaks in the San Juans. When I am aware of them, I have tried to include as many unofficial names as possible. In the headings, the unofficial names are given after designating the peak by elevation. Additionally, I also include in parenthesis the location of officially unnamed peaks in relationship to an officially named landmark in the area.

Exact elevations are not given for many peaks and passes in the San Juans. In those cases, I have approximated elevations by splitting the difference between contour lines. Almost all of the USGS maps for the San Juans are in the 7.5 minute series which have forty-foot contour lines. As a result, peaks such as the eastern summit of Point Pun is given an elevation of 13,180 when the highest contour line is 13,160. As a result, the approximated elevation should be no more than twenty vertical feet off from the exact elevation.

Clay Patton and Steve Kolarik on the Watch Crystal Crack near Durango, 5.10 plus. *Photo by David Kozak.*

RATING THE CLIMBS

It has been said that if you ask the same question of three lawyers, you will get three different opinions. The same principle applies to rating the difficulty of climbs.

The rating of a climb is ultimately a subjective decision. A rating is affected not only by the climber's ability, but also by the conditions under which the climb was made. There is, nevertheless, a method to the madness. The most frequently used rating system is the "Yosemite Decimal System."

The Yosemite Decimal System divides hiking and climbing into six different classes:

1. Hiking
2. Off-trail scrambling
3. Unroped climbing requiring the use of handholds
4. Roped climbing where a leader climbs without protection but gives the other climbers a belay
5. Roped climbing where the leader places protection
6. Aid or artificial climbing where equipment is used for advancement as well as protection

Classes 1 and 2 are what most climbers would otherwise term a "walkup." Within the San Juans, Handies, Sunshine, Redcloud, and Cirque would be examples of Class 1 and 2 climbs.

Class 3 climbing involves the use of handholds but is not so severe that most climbers feel the need for a rope. In the San Juans, Wilson Peak, Vermillion, and Eolus are good examples of third class climbing. The term "third class" climbing is sometimes used to describe how a climb was made rather than its difficulty. For example, if a climber is able to climb the north face of Storm King, which has been rated 5.7, without a rope, he is said to have climbed the route "third class." The difficulty and rating of the climb remain the same, but the climber's level of ability has allowed him to climb in a manner which most climbers would not consider.

Class 4 is one of the most subjective ratings. Class 4 climbs are on the borderline. In some instances, a member of a climbing party will desire the security of a rope whereas others will not. In the San Juans, Mount Wilson, El Diente, Middle Trinity, and Wetterhorn are probably best described as Class 4 climbs. Each of them contains a section on which experienced climbers feel capable of climbing without rope. A beginner or intermediate climber will, however, welcome the security of a rope belay on sections of these peaks.

Class 5 climbing is what is most frequently thought of when one is discussing "rock" or "technical" climbing. Class 5 was originally subdivided from 5.0 to 5.9. As the ability of climbers has increased, the range of subdivisions has likewise increased up to 5.13. In addition, 5.10, 5.11, 5.12, and 5.13 have been further divided into four subcategories from a to d. The north face of Storm King, Wham Ridge on Vestal, and the wall north of the saddle between West and Middle Trinity are examples of fifth class climbing.

Class 6 climbing is generally designated by a capital A and has been subdivided from A-1 through A-5, depending on the stability and load-bearing capacity of the aid placement and the length of the potential fall. Sunlight Spire, the Pope's Nose, and the 1968 route on the east face of Monitor are examples of aid climbing in the San Juans.

Under the Yosemite Decimal System, the rating given designates the difficulty of the hardest move on the climb. For example, if a five pitch climb has four pitches of 5.3 and one pitch of 5.8, the rating given to the climb is 5.8.

In order to give the climber an idea of the overall difficulty and length of time required on a climb, a Roman numeral is generally added to the rating which designates the "grade" of the climb. The grade ratings are as follows:

I. An hour or two
II. A few hours—half a day
III. Several hours—most of the day
IV. Long day
V. More than a day
VI. Two full days or more

There are no Grade VI climbs in the San Juans. The east face of Monitor and some of the routes on the Pope's Nose are the closest thing in the San Juans to a Grade V climb.

Another system of rating climbs which is mentioned in the text is the National Climbing Classification System (NCCS). The NCCS uses the same classifications for grade and aid climbing that are used by the Yosemite Decimal System. The only difference between the systems is the classification used for free climbing. Under the NCCS a capital F is followed by a letter. F-1 through F-3 correspond with Classes 1 through 4 of the Yosemite Decimal System. F-4 covers the range of 5.0 through 5.2. F-5 encompasses 5.3 and 5.4. F-6 encompasses 5.5 and 5.6. F-7, F-8, and F-9 correspond directly with 5.7, 5.8, and 5.9. F-10 corresponds with 5.10a and b, and F-11 corresponds with 5.10c and d.

Rating difficulty will inevitably be a somewhat controversial area. Although there is frequently debate over ratings, a consensus does usually emerge. The ratings for most of the harder routes in the San Juans are still in the consensus building stage. For that reason, I have not attempted to alter ratings given in climbing reports. When a route description is quoted from a report in a climbing periodical or journal, the rating given is that of the climbers making the report.

The San Juan Mountaineers taking a lunch stop on Kismet, 1932. Mel Griffiths (eating), Gordon Williams, and Dwight Lavender. *Photo by Mel Griffiths.*

THOSE WHO
CAME BEFORE:
An Overview of San Juan Climbing History

Many of the San Juan peaks were undoubtedly climbed by Indians. The San Juan Mountaineers reported that there was "direct evidence" that Indians had carried out hunting expeditions at least to an elevation of 13,000 feet on Uncompahgre Peak. Miners, also, certainly climbed many of the peaks in the area. The Hayden Survey, for example, reported finding prospect holes at 13,500 feet on Handies Peak in 1874. Unfortunately, we are in large measure left to speculate what the Indians and miners did or did not climb.

The first climbers to document their achievements were the early surveyors. The first excursions made by surveyors were in 1873. In that year, H.G. Prout climbed Engineer Mountain while with a Corps of Engineers party in the San Juans. Also in 1873, a Hayden Survey team made the first ascent of Stewart Peak. It was not until 1874, however, that the activities of the surveyors began in earnest and members of both the Hayden and Wheeler surveys began active exploration in the San Juans.

Frederick Endlich (left), Franklin Rhoda, and A.D. Wilson of the Hayden Survey, 1874. *W.H. Jackson photo, courtesy USGS.*

The Hayden Survey's exploits during the summer of 1874 are one of the most extraordinary chapters in the climbing history of the San Juans. The Hayden Survey team was headed by A.D. Wilson who had made the second ascent of Mount Rainier in 1870. The other members of the party were Frederick Endlich and Franklin Rhoda, the half-brother of A.D. Wilson, who wrote the "Report on the Topography of the San Juan Country" which gave a detailed chronicle of the Hayden team's exploits. Over the course of the summer of 1874, the Hayden party established fifty-four survey stations in the San Juans. A partial list of the peaks climbed by them includes Uncompahgre Peak, Sunshine Peak, Handies Peak, Rio Grande Pyramid, Mount Oso, Vermillion Peak, Mount Sneffels, and Mount Wilson. All but Rio Grande Pyramid were first recorded ascents. In addition to being the first party to climb many of the major peaks in the San Juans, the Hayden team had a lasting impact by naming many peaks in the area.

Although not as prolific as the Haydey Survey, the Wheeler Survey also made significant achievements in the San Juans over the course of the 1874 and 1875 seasons. The report of the Wheeler Survey's activities by William L. Marshall chronicles ascents of Uncompahgre Peak, Rio Grande Pyramid, Redcloud Peak, and several peaks in the La Platas. The Wheeler Survey's climbs on Rio Grande Pyramid and Redcloud Peak were first recorded ascents.

Beginning in the late 1800s and early 1900s, the San Juans began to attract climbers interested in scaling peaks solely for sport. In 1890, Percy Thomas from the Alpine Club of London, England, made a trip to the San Miguels and made a reconnaissance of Lizard Head and the first ascent of El Diente. Frederick Chapin also visited the area in 1890 and made an early ascent of Mount Sneffels and recorded his climb in the pages of *Appalachia*. The most ambitious of the early alpinists were William S. Cooper and John Hubbard. In 1906, Cooper visited

William S. Cooper and John V. Hubbard. Long's Peak Inn, 1906. In 1908 Cooper and Hubbard made first ascents of Pigeon, Arrow, and Vestal peaks. *Photo courtesy of William M. Bueler.*

the San Juans and climbed Kendall Mountain near Silverton to get a better view of the area. He was particularly struck by the view of the Needle Mountains. Cooper returned in 1908 with John Hubbard and made first ascents of Pigeon Peak, Arrow Peak, and Vestal Peak. In addition, they made early ascents of Vermillion, Mount Sneffels, Mount Wilson, and Uncompahgre Peak. Cooper and Hubbard were the first climbers who purposely sought out the most difficult peaks in the area.

One of the most historically significant climbs in the San Juans took place in 1920. In that year, Albert Ellingwood and Barton Hoag did what was previously thought impossible by climbing Lizard Head. At the time of its first ascent, Lizard Head was probably the most difficult climb in America. It is remarkable that the climb was achieved at that point considering the rudimentary equipment and protection devices available to Ellingwood and Hoag.

The next chapter in the climbing history of the San Juans belongs to the San Juan Mountaineers. In the early 1930s, a nucleus of strongly motivated climbers, including Dwight Lavender, Mel Griffiths, Gordon Williams, Chester Price, Henry McClintock, Frank McClintock, Lewis Geisecke, Forrest Greenfield, Carleton Long, and Everett Long, formed the San Juan Mountaineers. The San Juan Mountaineers made over fifty first ascents in the area. Some of the more notable achievements of the San Juan Mountaineers were three routes established during 1931, 1932, and 1933 on the north face of Sneffels, culminating in a direct route up the north face, the first ascent of Jagged Mountain, the first ascent of The Index, and the ascents of various pinnacles in the Sneffels area. In addition, the San Juan Mountaineers, in particular Mel Griffiths and Gordon Williams, began making ambitious winter climbs including Mount Sneffels.

The driving force in the organization was Dwight Lavender. Tragically, Lavender died of polio during the fall of 1934 at the age of twenty-three. During his short life, Lavender participated in over thirty first ascents with the San Juan Mountaineers. Lavender also wrote numerous articles on the group's exploits for *Trail and Timberline*, the *American Alpine Journal*, and the *British Mountaineering Journal*, for which he was serving as American Editor at the time of his death. As if this were not enough, Lavender co-authored with Carleton Long the *San Juan Mountaineer's Climber's Guide to Southwestern Colorado*.

Albert Ellingwood (left) and Carl Blaurock. Ellingwood with Barton Hoag made the first ascent of Lizard Head in 1920. Blaurock and William Ervin were the first climbers to climb all of Colorado's fourteeners. *Photo courtesy of Carl Blaurock.*

Frank (left) and Henry McClintock. The McClintocks teamed with various members of the San Juan Mountaineers and others to make numerous first ascents during the 1930s, 40s, and 50s. *Photo by Joe Merhar.*

John Speck, Joe Stettner, and Jack Fralick after the first ascent of the east face of Monitor Peak in 1947. *Photo courtesy of Joe Stettner.*

Looking up Wham Ridge during the first ascent in 1941. Rit Burrows (left) and Jim Patterson are shown climbing. *Photo by Werner Schnackenberg.*

Bob Ormes. Ormes participated in the first ascent of Chimney Rock, the first traverse of Needle Ridge, and the third ascent of Lizard Head. *Photo by Mel Griffiths.*

Spencer Swanger on the summit of Pigeon Peak. Swanger made the third reported ascent of Dallas Peak in 1976 and in so doing became the first person to climb the 100 highest peaks in Colorado. *Photo courtesy of Spencer Swanger.*

Lavender's achievements were staggering. Few have achieved during a full lifetime what he accomplished in a few brief years.

After the intense burst of activity generated by the San Juan Mountaineers in the early 1930s, a period of consolidation set in. Significant ascents were made during Colorado Mountain Club outings and by various members of the San Juan Mountaineers who remained active. Several significant climbs made during this era were Chimney Rock and the traverse of Needle Ridge by Mel Griffiths and Robert Ormes, the southeast chimney on Pigeon Peak by Frank McClintock, Henry McClintock, Mary McClintock, and Gordon Williams, and Wham Ridge on Vestal Peak by Rit Burrows, Werner Schnackenberg, and Jim Patterson.

In 1947, Joe Stettner, Jack Fralick, and John Speck made a remarkable ascent of the 1,200-foot east face of Monitor Peak. In many respects, this climb was well ahead of its time. While other American climbers were making severe climbs with the assistance of aid, Stettner, Fralick, and Speck free climbed (with the exception of two shoulder stands) what remains even by today's standards an extremely difficult route. Pitons were used for protection only, not for aid. Joe Stettner, who was forty-six years old at the time, had left his mark in the history of climbing in Colorado by climbing Stettner's Ledges on Longs Peak in 1927 and the north face of Lone Eagle Peak in 1933. Stettner felt that the east face of Monitor was far more difficult than his other climbs.

The Needles and Grenadiers became the focus of attention for climbers in the San Juans during the 1960s. Many different climbers were active. In 1962, John Ohrenschall and Doug Ward made technical ascents in the Grenadiers including the east faces of Arrow Peak and Electric Peak. Martin Etter, with various partners, climbed the north face of Coxcomb, the west face of Arrow Peak, the east face of Vestal, and the north face of Wildhorse Peak. George Bell was also active with several partners and made the first ascents of Sunlight Spire and Ominous Pinnacle. The east face of Monitor Peak was repeated by a more direct route in 1968 by Larry Dalke and Paul Stettner, Jr., Joe Stettner's nephew.

The 1960s also saw several difficult winter routes established in the Grenadiers. The Harvard Mountaineers climbed several difficult routes during their 1963 Christmas vacation. One which they missed, Wham Ridge, was climbed in January 1968.

During the 1970s, the emphasis on technical climbing in the

San Juans continued to center in the Grenadiers and Needles with various new routes made primarily on the north and east faces of the Grenadiers. Outside of the Grenadiers and Needles, the most significant ascents were made by Jeff Lowe and Paul Hogan on the north face of Wetterhorn Peak and Lowe and Larry Derby on the north face of Half Peak.

The 1970s and 1980s have seen a shift in emphasis. Many skilled climbers are devoting their energies toward developing difficult crag climbing areas near Telluride (Cracked Canyon, Ophir Wall, Ames Wall), Durango (The Watch Crystal), and the San Luis Valley. In addition, there is challenging ice climbing to be found in the Telluride and Ouray areas.

The San Juans will probably never again be on the cutting edge of American alpinism as they were when Ellingwood led Lizard Head or Stettner led Monitor's east face. There are, however, many hard mountaineering routes yet to be done. At present, for example, no one has reported an ascent of the east face of Pigeon, the north buttress of Turret, the south face of Gladstone, or a traverse of all of the summits on Jagged. These routes and many more will provide challenges for years to come.

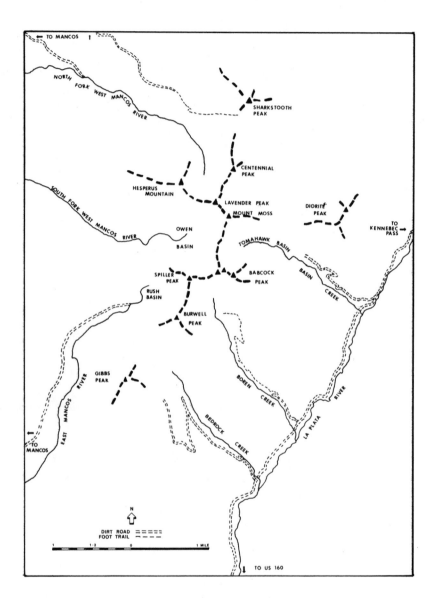

TO MANCOS

NORTH FORK WEST MANCOS RIVER

SHARKSTOOTH PEAK

CENTENNIAL PEAK

HESPERUS MOUNTAIN

SOUTH FORK WEST MANCOS RIVER

LAVENDER PEAK

MOUNT MOSS

DIORITE PEAK

TO KENNEBEC PASS

OWEN BASIN

TOMAHAWK BASIN

BASIN CREEK

SPILLER PEAK

BABCOCK PEAK

RUSH BASIN

BURWELL PEAK

GIBBS PEAK

EAST MANCOS RIVER

BOREN CREEK

BEDROCK CREEK

LA PLATA RIVER

TO MANCOS

N

DIRT ROAD ═════
FOOT TRAIL ─ ─ ─

1   1-2   0   1 MILE

TO US 160

LA PLATA MOUNTAINS

The La Platas are a distinct southwestern off-shoot of the San Juans. Although the La Platas were an area of intensive mining activity in the late 1800s, the peaks are seldom visited today except by local climbers and hikers. When climbing or hiking in the La Platas you can expect a pleasant day, away from the crowds.

For climbers, the principal attraction in the La Platas is a cluster of six 13,000-foot peaks: Hesperus Mountain, Lavender Peak, Centennial Peak, Mount Moss, Babcock Peak, and Spiller Peak. Hesperus is the highest peak in the group and is located northwest of the other peaks in the range. Hesperus is also one of the four sacred mountains of the Navajo Tribe. Named "Dibentsaa" by the Navajos, Hesperus is the Sacred Mountain of the North.

Lavender Peak is a spectacular bundle of pinnacles located on the ridge between Hesperus and Mount Moss. The northern flank of Lavender is covered by hundreds of sheer pinnacles.

To the northeast of Lavender lies Centennial Peak which in 1976 was named in honor of Colorado's 100th birthday. Centennial was formerly known as Banded Peak because it is composed of alternating horizontal layers of rust- and light-colored rock.

Mount Moss is an enjoyable climb which lies to the north of the rugged ridge which separates Owen Basin from Tomahawk Basin. To the south of this ridge lies Babcock Peak which consists of four separate and rugged summits. Directly west of Babcock, at the end of a high rugged ridge called "The Knife," lies Spiller Peak.

In addition to the 13,000-foot peaks, there are several 12,000-foot peaks of interest. To the north of the thirteeners lies Sharkstooth Peak; to the east is Diorite Peak; southeast of Spiller Peak are Burwell and Gibbs peaks. Each of these is an enjoyable day hike.

CLIMBING HISTORY

The early explorers were lured into the La Platas by the search for minerals. In the 1760s, the Spaniard Juan de Rivera led a prospecting party into the La Platas and found the silver for which the range is named.[1] By the 1870s, the La Platas were the scene of intensive mining and milling operations. Parrott City at the mouth of the La Plata Canyon was a boisterous mining town which was not only the county seat but also had the largest population in the county at that time.[2] Undoubtedly, most of the summits in the range were climbed by prospectors of that era.

The first survey team in the San Juans did not reach the La Platas but did take note of their presence. In his report for the 1874 Hayden Survey, Rhoda reported the view from the top of Engineer Mountain as follows:

> A group of pretty high peaks were seen to the southwest, called the La Plata Mountains. They were completely isolated from the main mass of the range by many miles of comparatively low land.[3]

The following year, William L. Marshall and J.C. Spiller of the Wheeler party made two topographical stations "upon prominent peaks of the Sierra La Plata."[4] The highest of the La

Plata peaks (presumably Hesperus) was also climbed by the party.

A separate Wheeler Survey party (there were six in all), headed by Lieutenant C.C. Morrison, also made a climb in the La Platas that same year. The Morrison party climbed what they called "Banded Peak" which would have been either Centennial or, more likely, Hesperus. On the descent, the chief topographer, Fred A. Clark, created some excitement when he "incautiously stamped his heels on the edge" of a large snowbank. Clark slipped and began sliding down the snow at the "velocity of a flash of light," with a spiked tripod in hand. Clark was able to plunge the tripod into the snow between his legs—"looking like a bearded baby riding a hobby horse"—and thereby halted his fall without damage other than the loss of the seat of his trousers.[5]

Hesperus Peak was climbed in 1876 by a Hayden Survey team which included William Henry Holmes. Holmes excelled both in geology and art. From the summit of Hesperus, Holmes made preliminary notes and sketches which he later transformed into a stunning drawing of the La Platas, which was published in *Hayden's Atlas of Colorado*.[6]

The La Platas were also the scene of climbs by the San Juan Mountaineers. On August 17, 1932, the west summit of Babcock Peak was traversed from north to south by J.E. Nelson and Carleton C. Long.[7] Lavender Peak, which was originally designated L1 by the San Juan Mountaineers, received its name in October 1975 in honor of one of the founders of the San Juan Mountaineers, Dwight Lavender. Designation as Lavender Peak was approved by the Board of Geographic Names, after receiving a recommendation from the Colorado Mountain Club Committee on Mountain Names which acted on the suggestion of Robert Ormes.

Notes

1. Bueler, *Roof of the Rockies*, p. 8.
2. *SJM Guide*, p. 182.
3. Rhoda, *Summits to Reach*, p. 65.
4. Wheeler, *Annual Report of the Chief of Engineers for 1876*, Appendix JJ, p. 82.

5. "The Wheeler Expedition in Southern Colorado," *Harpers, New Monthly Magazine*, May 1876, pp. 806-807.
6. Thomas M. Griffiths, *San Juan Country*, p. 208.
7. *SJM Guide*, p. 185.

ACCESS AND HIKING

Tomahawk Basin

The turnoff to La Plata Canyon and Tomahawk Basin is located one-half mile west of Hesperus near the Canyon Motel on U.S. 160. The turnoff is eleven miles west of Durango and seventeen miles east of Mancos. After turning north off U.S. 160, the first 4.7 miles of the road toward La Plata Canyon are paved. After 4.7 miles, the road turns to gravel and continues up the canyon. After a total of 10.8 miles from U.S. 160 (.4 after crossing Basin Creek), take a sharp switchback to the left. From this point, a rugged four-wheel drive road travels two miles up the north side of the drainage past the Tomahawk Mill to the old site of the Little Kate Mine. From the end of the road, a sketchy trail climbs up the right (north) side of the stream to the high basin. Tomahawk Basin provides excellent access to Diorite Peak, Mount Moss, and Babcock Peak. It is also a good means of access for Lavender Peak. The basin itself is a pleasant spot for either a picnic or half-day hike. The west end of the basin is separated from Owen Basin to the west by the sharply pinnacled ridge between the west summit of Babcock Peak and Mount Moss. Tomahawk Basin and Boren Basin to the south offer excellent spring skiing.

Boren Creek

The turnoff to Boren Creek is also located in La Plata Canyon.

Boren Basin as photographed by W.H. Jackson in 1875. Burwell Peak is on the left skyline. The summit of Spiller Peak is just left of the prominent notch on the right skyline. *Photo courtesy of USGS.*

The turnoff which leads up Boren Creek is located 8.5 miles up the La Plata Canyon Road from U.S. 160. The four-wheel drive road turns left shortly after the La Plata Canyon Road crosses Boren Creek. From the turnoff, a rugged four-wheel drive road leads into the upper basin. Even with four-wheel drive, the farthest I have ever made it up this road is .5 mile to Shaw Gulch. From Shaw Gulch, continue up the road on foot to the upper basin. The high basin provides good access to Burwell Peak, Spiller Peak, and Babcock Peak.

Bedrock Creek

Like Boren Creek, Bedrock Creek also drains the east side of the La Platas. The turnoff to Bedrock Creek is located 7.7 miles from U.S. 160, up La Plata Canyon. From the turnoff, two-wheel drive vehicles can go one and a half miles to a point where a branch of the road switchbacks sharply to the left. The road which goes straight ahead deadends just ahead at the Allard Mine. Four-wheel drive vehicles can make the sharp turn to the left and continue for another mile and a half to almost 11,000 feet. Bedrock Creek is the best means of access for climbing Gibbs Peak and also provides reasonable access for Burwell Peak.

Transfer Campground Road

Transfer Campground Road provides access to the La Platas from the west. The turnoff is located .3 mile north of Mancos, on Colorado 184. Turn off on the road marked for Jackson Reservoir and Transfer Campground. After 10.4 miles, turn right on a road just before Transfer Campground marked "Transfer Road 565." At 5.9 miles after the turnoff (16.3 miles from Mancos), a road turns to the right leading to the North Fork of the West Mancos River. If you are interested in climbing Hesperus Mountain, this is the best turnoff to take. After the turnoff, drive 2.2 miles on a rutted road to the North Fork of the West Mancos River where you are forced to start hiking because of a bridge washout. If you are interested in climbing Centennial Peak or Sharkstooth Peak, it is best to continue past the turnoff to Hesperus for an additional 2.5 miles where you will find another road turning off to the right, which is marked with a sign directing you to Sharkstooth Trail. This road will take you another 1.5 miles to the trailhead for Sharkstooth Trail.

Owen Basin

Owen Basin provides access to Hesperus, Lavender, Moss, and

the western and northwestern summits of Babcock and Spiller. There is not, however, a good means of gaining the basin by vehicle. You can only get close. The turnoff from U.S. 160 is located 2.5 miles east of Mancos and is marked by a sign directing you to Echo Basin. Follow the main road for 8.4 miles to a road junction and take the left branch toward Deer Lick Creek. At 3.6 miles after the junction (twelve miles from U.S. 160), a four-wheel drive road takes off to the left. Follow the four-wheel drive road for about two miles before it deadends in the lower portion of the drainage, below the upper basin. Another alternative is to stay on the main road at twelve miles and take a left turn at fourteen miles, where another four-wheel drive road takes you 1.3 miles just below the basin at the end of Spiller's west ridge. Although the second four-wheel drive road gains more elevation, it puts you out of position for anything other than Spiller.

Rush Basin

To gain Rush Basin, take the same turnoff as for Owen Basin. One mile after leaving U.S. 160, turn right onto a four-wheel drive road which takes you 10.5 miles to the Doyle Mine at 11,400 feet. From Rush Basin you can climb both Spiller and Burwell from the west.

CLIMBING ROUTES

Babcock Peak (13,149 feet)

Babcock Peak is comprised of four separate summits: east, middle, west, and northwest. Although closely clustered, it is very difficult to get from one summit to another. The elevation for the east summit is 13,149. The elevation for the other summits is not given on the USGS map. The northwest summit is at least 13,120 and the west summit is at least 13,080. The middle summit is the shortest at 13,040 plus, but is the most difficult to climb.

EAST SUMMIT — The east summit of Babcock, which is the easiest, is best climbed by its southeast ridge. The best approach for the southeast ridge is from high in Tomahawk Basin. From high in the basin, at about 12,000 or 12,200, contour around the northeast spur of the east summit and then head for the ridge. Once the ridge is gained, follow it directly to the top. At a couple of spots on the ridge, you will be forced to scramble left onto the south face before regaining the ridge. The east summit of Babcock Peak can also be gained by climbing the steep snow and ice couloir on the north face of the peak to the left (east) of the middle summit. The couloir is about forty degrees steep and five pitches long. The safest route to avoid rockfall in the couloir is to stay close to the right wall which affords points for placing protection once the couloir begins to ice up. From the top of the couloir there is one pitch of fourth class climbing which will place you on the south face, just below the summit.

MIDDLE SUMMIT — From the top of the couloir separating the middle summit and the east summit of Babcock Peak, a fifty- to sixty-foot wall of near-vertical, but well-broken up, rock separates you from easy scrambling to the summit. Rope and protection are recommended. Just to the north of the middle summit lies an amazing pinnacle. Slings near the top indicate that it has been climbed. It looks terrible.

NORTHWEST SUMMIT — The two routes to this summit both require fairly difficult scrambling over loose rock. From Tomahawk Basin, the best approach is to take the couloir right (west) of the middle summit to the saddle separating the middle and northeast summits. From the saddle, you can climb a steep, loose rock couloir to reach easier scrambling above. The saddle can also be reached from the Boren Creek side. From the Boren Creek side you can also take the couloir separating the northwest and west summits and then climb through some broken rock low in the couloir to gain the top of the cliffs.

WEST SUMMIT — The west summit can be climbed from the saddle connecting it to the northwest summit. Like the northwest summit, it is necessary to climb a steep, loose rock

Spire just north of the middle summit of Babcock Peak. *Photo by Robert F. Rosebrough.*

couloir near the top to reach the summit. From Tomahawk Basin, take the prominent couloir which starts at the base of the northwest summit and curves southwest. From the Boren Creek drainage, follow the couloir separating the northwest and west summits to reach the same saddle. The west summit is connected to Spiller Peak by a ridge called "The Knife." The best route on this ridge is on the very top except for the pinnacle near the summit of Spiller which is skirted to the north. The ridge involves some interesting scrambling, but most will not feel the need for a rope.

Ike Weaver climbing the "Knife" between Spiller Peak and the western summit of Babcock Peak. *Photo by Robert F. Rosebrough.*

Mount Moss (13,192 feet)

SOUTH RIDGE — The south ridge can be gained from Tomahawk Basin. Shortly before gaining the ridge, it is necessary to do some bouldering. Once on the ridge, you stay generally to the west until near the summit where the climb turns into a walkup.

Lavender Peak (13,180 feet approx.)

SOUTH FACE — Lavender Peak is comprised of two summits. The west summit is slightly higher. The summit is best gained by a third class scramble up a broad gully on the south face. At the notch between the two summits, be sure to stop and take note of the stunning pinnacle to the north.

Hesperus Mountain (13,232 feet)

NORTHWEST RIDGE — From the North Fork of the West Mancos River, hike south through the woods to gain the northwest ridge. Once on the ridge, follow it directly to the top. The lower portion of the ridge is a walkup. The upper 800 feet require a little scrambling but are not difficult.

Centennial Peak (13,062 feet)

NORTH RIDGE — The north ridge begins at the saddle between Centennial and Sharkstooth. Ernie Stromeyer reports that although the ridge is a little narrow in spots with some exposure, it is essentially a walkup. The view of Lavender from the summit of Centennial is particularly impressive.

Spiller Peak (13,123 feet)

SOUTHEAST FACE — The easiest route up Spiller is from the Boren Creek drainage. Once on the face, aim to gain the southern ridge which connects Spiller to Burwell. It is also possible to climb to the notch, just east of the summit, and then climb the last 200 feet on the north face.

EAST RIDGE — The east ridge of Spiller, which is called "The Knife," connects Spiller with the west summit of Babcock and is described there.

Diorite Peak (12,761 feet)

SOUTH FACE AND SOUTHWEST RIDGE — From the end of the Tomahawk Basin road, Stromeyer reports that you climb northeast up the steep slope to attain the ridge. On the face you will find parts scattered from an old airplane crash. Once on the ridge, you can walk it out to the summit.

Sharkstooth Peak (12,462 feet)

SOUTHWEST COULOIR — Sharkstooth lies just north of Centennial and both can easily be climbed together in a day. From the saddle between the two, Stromeyer suggests aiming for a couloir on the southwest face which leads you to a point just east of the summit. A small group is preferable because of the incredibly loose talus in the couloir.

Burwell Peak (12,664 feet)

EAST FACE — From high in the basin above Boren Creek, there are two variations on the east face. One variation is to cross Boren Creek at 10,600 feet and hike up the steep slopes just east of the summit. Shortly below the summit, you will gain the south ridge which leads directly to the summit. Another variation is to continue higher into the basin on the old mining road until it ends at about 11,200 feet. From that point, you can climb the east face to a point north of the summit and then follow the north ridge to the top.

Gibbs Peak (12,286 feet)

SOUTHEAST FACE — At the end of the Bedrock Creek road, hike directly up the southeast face and gain the ridge just to the right of the summit.

Dwight Lavender (left), Chester Price, and Forrest Greenfield, 1930. The col between Gladstone Peak and Mount Wilson is in the left background. The summit of Mount Wilson is just above Greenfield. *Photo by Lavender-Griffiths.*

SAN MIGUEL MOUNTAINS

The San Miguels offer a wide variety of climbing opportunities. The main cluster of the San Miguels is comprised of three 14,000-foot peaks, Mount Wilson, El Diente, and Wilson Peak, and one peak just under 14,000 feet, Gladstone Peak. Mount Wilson and El Diente have a well deserved reputation as two of the most difficult fourteeners to climb. The rugged, exposed ridge connecting Mount Wilson and El Diente is a "must climb" for serious mountaineers. Neighboring Wilson Peak is not as difficult as Mount Wilson and El Diente, but presents all the challenge the average climber cares for.

The almost fourteener, Gladstone Peak (13,913 feet) is an attractive peak which has been overlooked by climbers intent on the fourteeners. The south and west faces of Gladstone are 800-foot cliffs which offer the best hope for clean technical routes in the area.

Two or three miles southeast of the main cluster of peaks lurks the infamous Lizard Head, which has worked hard to gain its reputation as the most difficult and dangerous summit in the state of Colorado to attain. The history of climbing on Lizard Head is replete with stories of broken holds, rockfall, turned ankles, and climbing falls. In sharp contrast to the evil Lizard Head are the more rounded summits of Sunshine Mountain, directly east of the fourteeners, and Dolores Peak, Middle Peak, and Dunn Peak, to the west. Lone Cone completes the San Miguels. It sits in beautiful isolation several miles to the northwest of the other peaks in the range.

Climbing History

The history of climbing in the San Miguels begins with the Wheeler Survey in 1874. The Wheeler reports concerning Mount Wilson are conflicting. In Marshall's report for the 1875 field season, he wrote that Mount Wilson "was ascended in 1874 by Mr. Spiller, and in our notes was called Glacier Point."[1] An earlier report from the Wheeler Survey by Lieutenant Whipple in 1874 refers to "Glacier Peak, since named Meigs Peak, of the San Miguel Range, which the topographer of the party, Mr. Spiller, occupied with partial success."[2] What did Lieutenant Whipple mean by "partial success"? The Hayden Survey led by A.D. Wilson, after whom the peak was eventually named, did not climb Mount Wilson until late in the year. If in fact Spiller did climb Mount Wilson, his climb would have been a first ascent.

The question of whether Spiller attained the summit was probably resolved by a discovery made by William S. Cooper and John Hubbard in 1908. While downclimbing the difficult south ridge, Cooper and Hubbard passed over a particularly difficult spot in the ridge which forced them to use a rope for the first time during a summer of difficult climbing. Cooper reported that "just beyond it something in a crevice caught my eye. It proved to be an exceedingly rusty tin can; in it was a memorandum sheet very dirty and hard to read. I made out the name J. Calvert Stitler, and the date 1874; also Corps of Engineers, USA." The location of the tin can along the south ridge led Cooper to believe that "the man who left it was trying to climb Mount Wilson and that his nerve failed him at the cleft."[3] When these reports are taken as a whole, the logical conclusion is that Spiller (Stitler) did not reach the true summit of Mount Wilson.

The honor of the first ascent has generally been attributed to the Hayden Survey team which reached the summit of Mount Wilson on September 13, 1874. The Hayden team, which was comprised of A.D. Wilson, Franklin Rhoda, and Frederick Endlich, had developed a great deal of respect for Mount Wilson over the course of the summer. Rhoda reported:

> Only one peak of which we had any dread remained to be ascended, and that was Mt. Wilson. From various circumstances, we have reason to believe that this was higher than any station we had yet made, and from its rugged appearance we dreaded its ascent not a little.[4]

The Hayden Survey team approached Mount Wilson from the southeast and cut steps in a large steep snowbank to reach some "very steep and dangerous rock walls."[5] They straddled and slid across a great stone with its upper part wedged in a notch in the narrow south ridge. More difficult climbing on the south ridge led Rhoda to conclude that Mount Wilson was "by far the most dangerous of all the climbs of the summer."[6]

Early climbers on the north side of Mount Wilson found similar difficulties. In 1921, Carl Blaurock climbed the north face with Dudley T. Smith and William F. Ervin and reported that "on the last 200 feet we scrambled like scared cats along a backyard fence, . . ."[7]

Like Mount Wilson, neighboring El Diente suffered through an initial period of confusion concerning its first ascent. El Diente was first climbed by Percy Thomas and N.G. Douglas on September 2, 1890. Thomas and Douglas actually thought that they were climbing Mount Wilson.

Thomas was an Englishman and a member of the Alpine Club. His first climb in the area was of San Bernardo Mountain from which he viewed Lizard Head, which he described as a "marvelous rock-tooth." Thomas and Douglas, who was an assistant foreman at a local silver mine, set out to have a closer look at Lizard Head but upon reaching its base concluded that "our chance of making a successful ascent seemed as remote as anything could well be."[8]

After being frustrated by Lizard Head, Thomas and Douglas turned their attention toward what they thought was Mount Wilson. Although Thomas "fancied that climbing in the Rockies would be mere child's play by comparison with the Alps," he soon found "something more nearly akin to one or two well-known rock climbs than expected." All in all, Thomas was quite impressed by the area. He reported to the Alpine Club that "there are many untrodden peaks, and I will venture to say, many an interesting rock scramble, while if any member of the Club wishes to cover himself with glory let him climb, if he can, the Lizard's Head."

The fact that Thomas and Douglas had actually climbed El Diente rather than Mount Wilson was discovered by Dwight Lavender, who climbed El Diente on July 4, 1930 with Forrest Greenfield and Chester Price. At that time, Lavender assumed that they had made a first ascent since "a careful examination revealed no evidence of previous ascent."[9] After the climb, Lavender read an account of Percy Thomas's climb in the August 1891 volume of the *Alpine Journal.* Lavender and Thomas had both climbed the west ridge of El Diente and Lavender noted similarities in the description between his climb and the one reported by Thomas. In addition, Thomas had written of the "capital view of Mount Wilson" from Dunton. Lavender noted that although El Diente is quite striking when seen from Dunton, Mount Wilson "escapes all notice." Thomas did not discover his error upon reaching the summit of El Diente since "the view to the east was entirely blotted out, cutting off all possibility of seeing Mount Wilson."[10]

El Diente was given its name by Lavender, which means "The Tooth" in Spanish. Prior to being dubbed El Diente, the peak had been known locally as "The Jag" or "Montezuma Peak." In addition to naming El Diente, Lavender presented a successful case for including El Diente on the list as a separate fourteener. Lavender noted that El Diente did not meet some of the criteria set for determining separate summits, such as the combination of horizontal distance and vertical drop from the summit, but concluded that El Diente deserved separate status based on the difficulty of its ascent. He concluded that "I actually believe it would be impossible to ascend Mount Wilson and El Diente between sunrise and sunset even under the most favorable conditions."[11] While Lavender certainly overstated his argument, his point was well taken. Mount Wilson and El Diente are both difficult climbs connected by a treacherous ridge. The difficulty of climbing both Mount Wilson and El Diente, whether or not the connecting ridge is used, merits their separate status.

No one seems to know when or by whom Wilson Peak was first climbed. Blaurock, Ervin, and Smith climbed Wilson Peak in 1921 but it is generally assumed that it was climbed earlier by miners. Both Wilson Peak and Mount Wilson are named after A.D. Wilson of the Hayden Survey. Given Wilson's accomplishments as a surveyor and mountaineer, it is not hard to justify naming a 14,000-foot peak after him. Two fourteeners is another matter. Proposals have been made to rename both Mount Wilson and Wilson Peak, but the duplication continues.

Although less well traveled than its taller neighbors, Gladstone Peak is not without its own climbing history. The first recorded climb was by J.W. Emerson and F.B. Notestien in 1911. Emerson and Notestien's exact route is not known, but it is believed to be either the east face or northwest ridge. Twenty years later, a large party of twenty-four climbers led by Dwight Lavender and W.F. Ervin made the second ascent of Gladstone on August 20, 1931, during a joint outing of the Colorado Mountain Club and Appalachian Mountain Club.

Lizard Head has an intriguing climbing history. At the time of its first ascent in 1920 by Albert Ellingwood and Barton Hoag, Lizard Head was probably the hardest rock climb then completed in the United States. Armed with three soft iron pitons, hemp rope, and nailed boots, Ellingwood and Hoag made a couple of abortive attempts on cracks near the southwest corner before rounding the corner to the west face. Ellingwood reported that "most of the enticing small holds crumbled at a touch, and large masses of the loosely compacted pebbles would topple dangerously at a slight pull."[12] In spite of the difficulties, they struggled up and placed two of their rustic pitons in the lower cliff, saving one for the higher cliffs.

After spending about a half hour on top of the summit, Ellingwood and Hoag began an epic descent. Ellingwood's rope became stuck on the lower cliff. As he shook it, a rock came loose and hit him on top of the head, almost knocking him from the wall. Hoag was also hit by rockfall but was on secure footing at the time. After more effort, they had to abandon the rope and begin downclimbing. Ellingwood reported that Hoag "slipped and, leaving a section of his pants behind, drifted relentlessly downward until the wall became vertical and then jumped (perhaps fifteen feet) to the rocks below. I followed with more caution, regretfully saying goodbye to my rope that had served me well for five good seasons."[13]

Lizard Head Peak. *Photo by Thomas S. Sawyer.*

Ellingwood and Hoag's climb was well ahead of its time. This is reflected in the comments of Harold G. Wilm who made the second ascent on June 9, 1929 with Dobson West. Referring to Ellingwood, Wilm noted:

> At the time, it was considered an impossible feat, and little credence was given his performance by many who knew the peak. For some time, therefore, Dobson West and I had planned a second ascent, chiefly as a proof of his climb, but also as a mountaineering stunt of our own.[14]

Wilm and West did in fact confirm the first ascent by retrieving Ellingwood's old rope and finding his old rusty pitons still in place. Several more ascents of Lizard Head were made during the 1931 joint outing by members of the Colorado and Appalachian Mountain clubs. Since the early efforts, interest in Lizard Head has waned. The horror stories have taken their toll.

Nevertheless, a few brave souls have persisted. The first winter

The airy summit of Lizard Head. *Photo by Stuart Krebs.*

Don Doucette leading the first pitch on Lizard Head during the first winter ascent in January 1970. *Photo by R.J. Campbell.*

Art Howells leading the last pitch on Lizard Head during the first winter ascent in January 1970. *Photo by R.J. Campbell.*

ascent of Lizard Head was made on January 18, 1970, by a strong party from Colorado Springs which consisted of Art Howells, Mike Dudley, Don Doucette, Chuck Behrensmeyer, R.J. Campbell, and Fletcher Smith. Although the first 100 feet of the climb had snow on all the holds, they made excellent time and got on and off the summit cone in about four hours.[15]

Although Lone Cone was not climbed by the Wheeler Survey, Marshall reported that "it is the most beautiful peak I have ever seen. It is entirely detached from the other mountains, and rises, a solitary, graceful peak, 3,000 feet above its base. It was named by me West Point. This is the last peak to the west [in Colorado]."[16] It is unknown who made the first ascent of Lone Cone, but the first recorded ascent of the difficult north face was made by Dwight and David Lavender on September 4, 1931.[17] Dwight Lavender felt that the north face was "an excellent climb, one of the best in the southwestern Colorado Rockies."[18] Dwight Lavender and R.L. Phillippi also made an early ascent of Sunshine Mountain on August 18, 1931.[19] The first recorded ascent of Dunn Peak, which was then known as Middle Peak, was made by Ira Y. Meyers on August 28, 1912.[20] First ascent information for Dolores Peak and Middle Peak is unavailable.

Notes

1. Wheeler, *Annual Report of the Chief of Engineers for 1876*, Appendix IV, p. 99.
2. Hart, *Fourteen Thousand Feet*, p. 31.
3. William S. Cooper's unpublished manuscript entitled "Mountains," p. 82.
4. Rhoda, *Summits to Reach*, p. 80.
5. *Ibid.*, p. 81.
6. *Ibid.*, p. 83.
7. *T & T*, January 1922.
8. Thomas, "Mountaineering in Southern Colorado," *Alpine Journal*, Vol. XV, August 1891, p. 483.
9. *T & T*, September 1930.
10. *T & T*, September 1931.
11. *T & T*, May 1931.
12. Albert L. Ellingwood, *Outing Magazine*, November 1921, p. 54.

13. *Ibid.*, p. 92.

14. *T & T*, August 1931.

15. *Climbing*, September 1970, p. 23. Personal correspondence, R.J. Campbell.

16. Wheeler, *Annual Report of the Chief of Engineers for 1876*, Appendix IV, p. 99.

17. *SJM Guide*, p. 109.

18. *T & T*, October 1931.

19. *SJM Guide*, p. 122.

20. *Ibid.*, p. 107.

ACCESS AND HIKING

Silver Pick Basin

Silver Pick Basin is a popular point of access for climbers interested in knocking off the area's fourteeners. The basin is reached by following the Silver Pick Road which leaves Colorado 145 6.5 miles east of Placerville and 9.5 miles west of Telluride (six miles west of the Telluride exit on 145). After crossing the bridge over the San Miguel River, the road follows Big Bear Creek south four miles to a marked junction. Turn right and continue in a southerly direction for 3.5 miles where you get a view of the basin at about 11,000 feet.

The road used to be closed by a locked metal gate a mile lower but in recent years the gate has not been locked. Four-wheel drives can make the sharp switchback at 11,000 feet and continue up the basin until stopped by snow or rock slides. Four-wheel drive is recommended for this road, although many two-wheel drive vehicles have made it to the basin at 11,000 feet. This route can be difficult when wet since it tends to get slick and it is necessary to cross a stream which swells during storms. It is also notorious for eating more than its fair share of tires.

After reaching the basin, there are a couple of hiking options. The first involves hiking up the old road to the Silver Pick Mine

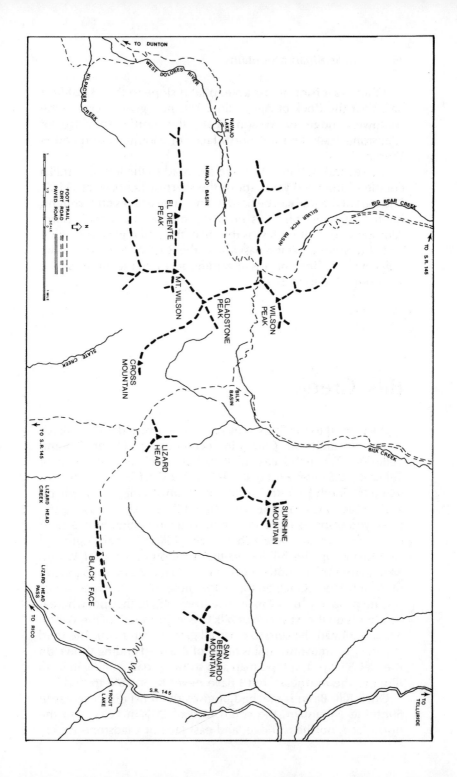

and then traversing across a steep talus slope to the 13,020-foot pass near the Rock of Ages Mine. This pass gives access to the southwest ridge of Wilson Peak, the northwest ridge of Gladstone Peak, and the north faces of Mount Wilson and El Diente.

The second option is to leave the road to the left on a trail a couple of hundred yards above the sharp switchback at 11,000. The start of the trail can be hard to find since it takes off through a jumble of talus, but it is normally marked by a rock cairn. Although not quite as fast as the road, the trail is pleasant hiking and also winds up at the pass above the Rock of Ages Mine. The trail is a more direct means of gaining access to the routes on the west side of Wilson Peak.

Bilk Creek

The turnoff to the Bilk Creek road (four-wheel drive required) is also located on Colorado 145 between Placerville and Telluride. Ten miles east of Placerville and six miles west of Telluride (2.5 miles west of the Telluride exit), turn off on the exit marked "South Fork Rd." After one-tenth of a mile, turn right on a dirt road and cross the San Miguel River. After crossing the river, you come to a junction where you must either turn left and cross Bilk Creek or take a sharp right. Take the sharp right and switchback up the hillside to the meadows on top of Wilson Mesa. From the turnoff on Colorado 145 it is 2.6 miles to the top of Wilson Mesa. Once on top of the mesa follow the road across private property for 5.2 miles (7.8 from 145) to the spot where it deadends on the west side of Bilk Creek, just south of the Wilson Mesa trailhead. Be sure to close all gates behind you. The road leaves you almost two miles north of the road ending shown on the USGS map. The topo map also shows a road coming in from Ilium to the northeast, but I have never been able to find it.

Once Bilk Basin is reached, it gives the most direct access to Sunshine Mountain, the south face of Wilson Peak, and the north face, northeast ridge, and east face of Gladstone Peak.

Lizard Head Creek Trail

Lizard Head Creek Trail starts two miles southwest of Lizard Head Pass on Colorado 145 at 10,000 feet. The trail heads northwest for one and a half miles where it turns directly north for two miles and joins the Lizard Head Trail at about 11,900 feet. From the junction of the two trails, there is an easy contour one-third of a mile northwest to the saddle between Cross Mountain and Lizard Head. To the north lies Bilk Basin and Bilk Creek Trail. This is the most direct approach for Lizard Head and Cross Mountain. It is also a feasible approach for the east face of Gladstone Peak. It does make a rather long day to climb Gladstone by this route and involves losing and then regaining 400 feet from the saddle between Cross Mountain and Lizard Head down into Bilk Basin.

Lizard Head Trail

This trail starts at Lizard Head Pass and contours northeast for one and one-half miles before it turns west and switchbacks one and one-miles west to the top of Black Face. From there it heads due west and then northwest for 3.5 miles to the 11,979-foot pass between Lizard Head and Cross Mountain. This is a beautiful hiking trail but is a little too indirect to be used as access for climbing. Although the USGS and Forest Service maps indicate that the trail starts near Trout Lake on Colorado 145, I have never been able to find a trailhead there. Apparently the trail was rerouted to avoid the vertical gain required by a start near Trout Lake.

Navajo Lake Trail

This is a popular trail which approaches the highest peaks in

Rest stop at the Rock of Ages Mine high in Navajo Basin. Gladstone Peak is just left of center, and Mount Wilson is on the right. *Photo by Ernie Stromeyer.*

the San Miguel Range from the southwest. The trailhead can be reached from several different directions. One way is to turn off Colorado 145 thirteen miles northeast of Dolores and follow a well-maintained gravel road for twenty-three miles to Dunton. Upon reaching Dunton, continue another 2.5 miles to Burro Bridge which crosses the West Dolores River. After crossing Burro Bridge, the road switches back and heads north to the well-marked trailhead. Another way to reach the trailhead is via the Dunton Road which leaves Colorado 145 seven miles northeast of Rico and 10.5 miles southeast of Ophir. After 4.5 miles you will reach the Meadows. Another three miles will bring you to the Navajo Lake trailhead. The trail starts at about 9,300 feet and follows the east side of the West Dolores River before crossing the river and passing through some large meadows. From the meadows there are excellent views of Dolores Peak to the west and El Diente to the east. Once past the meadows, the trail climbs through the forest to timberline at 11,400 feet and then drops down to Navajo Lake at 11,154 feet. The trail is slightly under five miles long from the trailhead to Navajo Lake.

The Navajo Lake Trail gives excellent access to the west ridge and north face of El Diente. After hiking higher into Navajo Basin, the north face of Mount Wilson, the northwest ridge and west face of Gladstone, and the southwest ridge of Wilson Peak are also accessible. The Navajo Lake Trail also can be used as access to Dolores Peak by turning northwest at the meadows about one and one-quarter miles up the trail.

Kilpacker Creek

Jim Gehres reports that Kilpacker Creek provides an alternate means of access to Mount Wilson and El Diente. The advantage to this approach is that the backpack is easier than the Navajo Lake Trail, being about four miles and a 1,000-foot elevation gain rather than five miles and 2,100 feet vertical. The disadvantage is that there is not a clear trail going to the campsite in the upper drainage. The initial objective is to reach the Meadows on the Dunton Road between Dunton and Colorado 145. Just west of a seemingly abandoned ranch house (Morgan Camp on the USGS map) at 10,100 feet, the road starts to lose elevation and eventually switchbacks down at this point. Take a fairly obscure side road which angles to the right (assuming you are headed west). You are forced to park a very short distance along this road where it is barricaded to motor vehicles. From there, the trail, at first an abandoned jeep road, heads west for one mile and then turns north for one and one-half miles, gaining very little elevation, and crosses Kilpacker Creek. Roughly two city blocks before it crosses the creek, at an elevation of 10,400 feet, where it starts to head slightly downhill, there is an obscure path leading to the right up the south bank of Kilpacker Creek. Follow this path until it crosses the creek in less than a mile, and then head up the north bank of the creek across grassy meadows for less than a mile. There is a good camp spot located in pine trees beneath a spectacular waterfall at about 11,000 feet.

Fish Creek

Fish Creek provides the most direct access to Dolores, Middle, and Dunn peaks. About one-half mile north of Dunton, a well-maintained gravel road heads northwest for Groundhog Reservoir. Four miles from the turnoff, you will reach Fish Creek. With four-wheel drive you can continue up the Fish Creek drainage almost one-half mile. If you are interested in the southwest face of Dolores Peak, take the right-hand turn at .3 mile.

West Beaver Creek Road

The West Beaver Creek Road is the approach for Lone Cone. The starting point is located 1.5 miles east of Norwood on Colorado 145. From the turnoff, travel 10.7 miles south on pavement, then turn left and follow the sign to Beaver Park. Turn right at mile 14.1. At mile 19.2, turn right onto West Beaver Creek Road, which you follow until taking another right at mile 20.9 onto Forest Road 612. Road 612 will take you to a point about 1.5 miles northeast of Lone Cone's summit and puts you in position to climb the northwest ridge, northeast ridge, or north face of Lone Cone. Ernie Stromeyer tells me that you can reach the same spot by turning right on the Galloway Road at mile 16.5. Four-wheel drive helps on either approach. You can also reach the West Beaver Creek Road from the southeast by taking the Groundhog Reservoir Road just north of Dunton and then heading north toward Beaver Park. The southeastern approach involves more dirt road than most people care to drive.

CLIMBING ROUTES

Wilson Peak (14,017 feet)

WEST FACE — This is the most direct route on Wilson Peak. At 12,800 feet, the trail up Silver Pick Basin makes a ninety-degree turn and begins to contour south toward the pass above the Rock of Ages Mine. Rather than turning right and contouring toward the pass, continue up into the basin below the west face of Wilson Peak. Early in the year this basin usually has a large snowbank. Once in the basin there are several variations which lead to the southwest ridge and then to the summit. Later in the year, expect to encounter talus and loose rock.

It is also possible to gain the southwest ridge from the west by continuing on the Silver Pick Basin trail a short distance after it turns south at 12,800 feet and then climbing left, up the prominent gully which meets the southwest ridge at 13,700 feet. Although passable, this gully is a jumble of loose rock.

SOUTHWEST RIDGE — From the Silver Pick Basin area, climb to the 13,020-foot pass overlooking the Rock of Ages Mine. From the pass, contour to the ridge between Wilson Peak and Gladstone. From this ridge a trail of sorts traverses up the right (east) side of the southwest ridge and attains the ridge itself at about 13,400 feet. It is possible to gain the southwest ridge earlier but this involves significantly more difficult climbing and some loss of elevation once the ridge is gained. Once on the ridge, you will be forced to make a short downclimb on the west side, shortly below the summit, which involves some exposure. A steep but well-broken up face leads back to the ridge and summit.

SOUTH FACE — Hal Brown reports that in late spring and early summer the south face is a steep snow climb. From the old miner's cabin in Bilk Basin at 12,800, head directly up the face to gain the southwest ridge. Once the snow is gone, the route is covered by loose talus and, therefore, loses its attraction.

Wilson Peak. *Photo by Thomas S. Sawyer.*

Mount Wilson (14,246 feet)

NORTH FACE — The north face is accessible either by downclimbing 600 feet from the pass connecting Silver Pick Basin and Navajo Basin or by climbing past Navajo Lake, high into Navajo Basin. Until shortly below the summit, the north face is not particularly difficult. Although it does involve a little bit of scrambling, there are several variations which lead toward the final summit ridge. The last ridge section involves exposed and at times precarious climbing along a thin ridge which, although it appears unstable, is relatively firm.

SOUTH FACE — The lower south face involves a straightforward but steep climb. As with the north face, the difficulties begin near the top. Once the top of the south face is gained, it is necessary to either traverse or climb over the five points directly south of the main summit. Each of the five points exceeds 14,000 feet and the climb from the first point to the true summit takes time. Most climbers have found the traverse to the

Mount Wilson during October storm. *Photo taken from Gladstone Peak by Robert F. Rosebrough.*

Craig Pirlot climbing Mount Wilson's summit ridge.
Photo by Jay Mason.

east to be the better alternative. The final section of the south ridge, just below the summit, presents some difficulty. Rhoda of the Hayden Survey described a notch in the ridge "filled in by a great stone, with its upper part wedge-shaped." The survey team passed this wedge by "straddling it and sliding ourselves carefully across." The ridge does not ease up at this point, as Rhoda described further problems with "a steep rock-wall of loose shelving rock."

SOUTHEAST FACE — Head directly up the southeast face toward the large snowbank. After reaching the saddle between Five Points and the true summit, climb the south ridge below the summit which is described in the south face description.

MOUNT WILSON-EL DIENTE RIDGE — This ridge is a classic. It is undoubtedly one of the most difficult ridges between fourteeners. The ridge is .8 mile long. The low point is 346 vertical feet below Mount Wilson and 259 feet below El Diente. When

The Mount Wilson-El Diente ridge as viewed from the summit of Mount Wilson. *Photo by Robert F. Rosebrough.*

both fourteeners are climbed together, via the ridge, it is best to climb Mount Wilson first. The first two-thirds of the ridge involves some scrambling and exposure but is not unreasonably difficult. At this point, however, you are confronted with a thirty-foot rappel or a severe downclimb. After the rappel, it is best to drop off the ridge to the south (left) to avoid a series of rock pinnacles called the Organ Pipes before regaining the ridge shortly below the summit. The rock on the ridge is hard, highly fractured, and fairly stable.

El Diente (14,159 feet)

WEST RIDGE — The west ridge can be gained either from Navajo Lake to the north or Kilpacker Creek Basin to the south. Once on the ridge, follow it to the summit. Before reaching the summit you will be forced south from the ridge by a rock buttress and then north by a narrow spot.

NORTH FACE— From Navajo Lake Basin, there are a couple of routes. One follows the broad couloir directly north of the summit. The other climbs the steep snowfield to gain the low point on the Mount Wilson-El Diente ridge and then follows the ridge route described under Mount Wilson.

SOUTH FACE — One look at the south face leaves no doubt that this is a serious proposition. The July 1942 issue of *Trail and Timberline* reports that the second group to climb the south face "had to do some tough rock work before reaching the summit." An easier route climbs the south face directly below the low point on the Mount Wilson-El Diente ridge and then follows the Mount Wilson-El Diente ridge route to the top.

Gladstone Peak (13,913 feet)

NORTHWEST RIDGE — Gain the ridge between Gladstone and Wilson Peak at its lowest point and follow it directly to the summit. This is a moderate climb but care should be taken because of loose rock. In *Colorado's High Thirteeners*, Garratt and Martin report that "the climbing is slow because of the large boulders."

EAST FACE — Climb the south (left) side of the face and aim to meet the southeast ridge at about 13,500 feet so as to avoid the steep band of cliffs at this level on the north (right) side of the face. There is a breathtaking view of Gladstone's south face and the east face of Mount Wilson from the southeast ridge. Traverse over loose rock to the northeast ridge about 200 to 300 feet from the top and follow the northeast ridge to the summit.

NORTH FACE — The lower portion of the north face is covered by the permanent snowfield named Gladstone Glacier by the San Juan Mountaineers. In his *Guide to the Colorado Mountains*, Ormes reports that Gladstone "makes a steep snow climb from the north." An ice ax is essential; crampons would also be helpful, particularly later in the year.

SOUTHWEST RIDGE — This is the steep, rugged ridge connecting Gladstone to Mount Wilson. George Bell reports encountering "a face of solid rock followed by a short very loose section above."

Lizard Head (13,113 feet)

WEST FACE — Several written accounts report that the route starts up a rotten chimney just north of the southwest corner. The west face is divided into two cliffs. Follow the rotten chimney for about eighty feet. Angle left over a large difficult slab to the top of the first cliff. From the top of the first cliff there is an easy section to the bottom of the second cliff. At this point the route follows a 100-foot vertical chimney. The lower section of the chimney is interrupted by a difficult overhang. Once past the overhang the chimney eases up a bit. Continue directly up the chimney to the easy but loose summit slopes. The large slab on the lower cliff above the eighty-foot belay stance is considered the crux. In their history of technical climbing in Colorado, *Climb*, Bob Godfrey and Dudley Chelton quote Larry Dalke as grading the crux "at least 5.7 and perhaps harder."

Sunshine Mountain (12,930 feet)

NORTHWEST RIDGE — This climb starts at 10,000 feet where the old Bilk Creek Road crosses the stream. Climb up the north side of the stream, past the waterfalls to timberline at 10,800 feet. From timberline, traverse left to gain the northwest ridge which curves its way to the summit.

Dolores Peak (13,290 feet)

EAST FACE — This is the most accessible route when climbed from Navajo Lake Trail. After hiking a mile and one-quarter up Navajo Trail to the large meadows, leave the trail and head northwest for two miles toward the east face. Once at timberline, you can pick between many variations which lead to the summit.

SOUTHWEST FACE — From the Fish Creek drainage, follow the clearing toward the southwest face which leads you to the summit over loose scree and talus.

NORTH FACE — The north face is a large talus field which rises above the gentle saddle (12,580) between Dolores and Middle peaks. To reach the saddle, take the right (east) drainage up Fish Creek. The saddle affords excellent views of the fourteeners and Gladstone surrounding Navajo Basin to the east.

Dunn Peak (12,595 feet)

NORTH RIDGE — The north ridge is an easy snow climb in late spring or early summer. Once the snow is gone, the route is composed of small but fairly stable scree.

SOUTH FACE — The south face is a grind over loose scree. The romp downhill is fun.

Middle Peak (13,261 feet)

In the 1930s, Middle Peak was known as Dolores Peak. At some point thereafter, the names of Dolores, Middle, and Dunn peaks were changed to their present designations. On the Dolores Peak quadrangle, the summit of Middle Peak is marked at the northwest point on the long summit ridge. Actually a point on the ridge to the southeast is higher (at least 13,280). A metal plate is still wired to the summit cairn of Middle Peak advising you that you have climbed "Dolores Peak."

SOUTHEAST FACE — The southeast face is a pleasant walkup from the saddle separating Dolores and Middle peaks.

SOUTHWEST RIDGE — The southwest ridge is gained by following the main fork of Fish Creek to the left (west) toward the saddle between Dunn and Middle peaks. Take your time on the loose rocky section in the middle of the ridge.

Lone Cone (12,613 feet)

NORTHEAST RIDGE — Ernie Stromeyer reports that the ridge is made up of small spires which you must work your way over and around. It is also loose and exposed. Some parties will prefer the security of a rope while on the ridge. The route ends up on the slabs of the east face which are welcomed after the loose ridge.

NORTHWEST RIDGE — The northwest ridge is frequently used as a descent route for parties who have climbed the northeast ridge. It is both easier and less exposed than the northeast ridge.

Dwight Lavender giving Lewis Giesecke a shoulder stand on Kismet during the early 1930s. *Photo by Mel Griffiths.*

SNEFFELS RANGE

The Sneffels Range is, with the exception of the Needles-Grenadiers, the largest concentration of high, rugged peaks in the San Juans. The monarch of the range, Mount Sneffels, is a beautiful mountain and certainly one of the most interesting not only in the San Juans but in Colorado.

Sneffels offers an excellent variety of climbing from the moderate standard route up the southeast couloir to the rugged north face with its steep snow and ice couloirs.

Other interesting aspects of Sneffels are the rock pinnacles which flank its northwest and western ridges. On the lower portion of the northwest ridge, three spectacular pinnacles, The Hand, The Penguin, and The Thumb are closely clustered. Higher on the ridge is the prominent Purgatory Point. To the southwest lie the Wolf's Tooth, Blue Needle, and The Monolith.

Although Sneffels is the only 14,000-foot peak in the group, both Dallas Peak and Teakettle Mountain exceed 13,800 feet in elevation. Dallas is regarded by many climbers to be the most difficult of the high peaks in Colorado to climb. Although not quite as difficult as Dallas, Teakettle is also a very challenging climb. The summit pinnacle of Teakettle is an interesting geological formation with the handle of the teakettle formed by a perfectly circular hole.

Teakettle is one of the series of high peaks which extend east from Mount Sneffels to the north of Yankee Boy Basin. Just east of Sneffels lies Kismet. Kismet is separated from Mount Sneffels to the west by Scree Col and Cirque Mountain to the east by Dike Col. The ridge culminates to the east with Potosi, whose flat summit is guarded by spectacular 200-foot cliffs.

Yankee Boy Basin is bounded on the south by Gilpin Peak, Mount Emma, and Mendota Peak. Spectacular St. Sophia Ridge is a rugged line of rotten rock pinnacles which separates Mount Emma and Mendota Peak.

Dallas Peak, West Dallas Peak, and T O lie to the west of Gilpin Peak at the head of Blue Lakes Basin.

CLIMBING HISTORY

Undoubtedly, many peaks in the Sneffels group were climbed by miners who did not record their exploits. During a climb of Gilpin Peak in 1952, John Filsinger found an old hand-forged miner's pick just below the summit. The first recorded ascent in the area was Mount Sneffels by the Hayden Survey on September 10, 1874. The Hayden Survey team reached the southwest ridge which they "had to climb with care" since it "was quite steep in some places."[1]

Sneffels' present name is a corruption of the name given it by the Hayden Survey after the Icelandic volcano described in Jules Verne's *Journey to the Center of the Earth.* Although Rhoda's report does not mention the naming of Sneffels, Dr. Endlich of the Hayden team described the event to Frederick S. Chapin who reported it as follows in the December 1890 issue of *Appalachia*:

> Looking down upon the north side, one sees a deep gulf which is described by Lt. Rhoda in Hayden Survey. This recalls the matter of naming the peak. Dr. Endlich was standing in the abyss with one companion, who compared it to the great hole described by Jules Verne in "Journey to

the Center of the Earth." Endlich agreed with him, and pointed to the great peak above exclaiming "there's Snaefell!" Thus the peak got its name, though it is pronounced by the people of the valley as Sneffels and is so written on the maps, and in the tables of the coast survey.

In 1884, Sneffels was climbed by Alexander Taylor, who was a contractor and prospector from Ouray. Taylor also led Frederick Chapin up the southeast couloir in 1890, which is now the standard route.

The first recorded ascent of a peak in the group, other than Sneffels, was made in August 1929. At that time, Charles Rolfe and Alonzo Hartman climbed Teakettle Mountain. Although Rolfe and Hartman were with a party of four, the other two climbers stopped at the base of the difficult summit pinnacle. Hartman and Rolfe did not leave a cairn on the summit. They did, however, leave a small jar at the base of the pinnacle containing the names of the party.[2]

In the early 1930s, the Sneffels Range was actively climbed by the San Juan Mountaineers. One of the primary objectives of the San Juan Mountaineers was the north face of Sneffels which they climbed by different routes in 1931, 1932, and 1933.

In his report of the 1931 climb, Dwight Lavender noted that "the taunting north face of Mount Sneffels, untrodden by men, had beckoned to us for years."[3]

Lavender, Melvin Griffiths, Charles Kane, and Gordon Williams climbed the lower portion of the north face on July 16, 1931, by the east couloir. They followed the east couloir to the northeast arete which they then followed to the summit. After the climb Lavender noted:

> I might add as an afterthought that the north face of Sneffels offers some of the best and most varied climbing in the state; it can be classed with such difficult local climbs as the Coxcomb, Vermillion Peak, by the southwest arete, Mt. Wilson by the west arete ("a more difficult climb than the Capital knife edge"), and there are bits on the peak fully as difficult to overcome as the Lizard Head.[4]

On July 6, 1932, Lavender, Griffiths, and Williams returned to the north face and chose a route up the right or northwest couloir. "The couloir proved to be a veritable hell of snow: hard snow, crusted snow, soft snow, and soggy snow."[5]

The north face of Mount Sneffels from Blaine Basin. *Photo by Robert F. Rosebrough.*

The San Juan Mountaineers achieved their goal of a direct route on the north face in 1933. In August of that year Lavender, Griffiths, Lewis Giesecke, Dr. H.L. McClintock, Mary McClintock, and Frank McClintock climbed directly up to the great cliff which splits the center of the face. The lower portion of the rock face presented the greatest difficulties. At one point the party narrowly avoided disaster. Griffiths was leading and had taken a detour around an overhang. Lavender was climbing behind Griffiths and the two climbers were having difficulty hearing each other. Griffiths thought that Lavender was planning to climb the overhang directly. Unknown to Griffiths, who was giving a shoulder belay, Lavender was actually planning to do a pendulum swing to a crack. Griffiths reported that

> before I was ready, his full weight came swinging down on the rope, and I was fighting to keep my balance on the narrow ledge. For an instant I let the rope slide over my shoulder while I dug in my heels. Then I clamped down tight. The shock brought me half to my knees before I could stop his fall. A moment later he was dangling free below the overhang, and I was thanking my lucky stars that we had spent some hours during the summer in belay practice.[6]

After the early difficulties, the group made better time higher on the face and reached the summit after ten hours of climbing.

Another objective of the San Juan Mountaineers was the pinnacles to the northwest and west of Sneffels. The first of the pinnacles to be climbed was The Hand in July 1932, by Williams, Griffiths, and Lavender. They chose the name because "it slightly resembles the palm of a hand, with the thumb to the south and the tips of the fingers overhanging a little to the east."[7] On The Hand, they climbed up a ledge on the west side to a "small gendarme." A traverse where "the only possible route lay across the balls of our fingers" led to the summit.[8]

During the 1934 Summer Outing of the Colorado Mountain Club, several more of the pinnacles were climbed. John Seerley and Robert Thallon climbed Blue Needle. Lewis Giesecke and Carleton Long climbed The Monolith. The Penguin was climbed by Dwight Lavender and John Seerley. The Wolf's Tooth and The Thumb were climbed the year before by Lavender, Giesecke, and Griffiths. The Wolf's Tooth was climbed by a "solid jam chimney on the south face."[9]

Although the San Juan Mountaineers conducted a

Dwight Lavender and Carleton Long (white) climbing on chimney on the Wolf's Tooth during the early 1930s. *Photo by Lavender-Griffiths.*

reconnaissance of Purgatory Point, it appears to be the only major pinnacle on the northwest or west side of Mount Sneffels which they did not climb in the early 1930s. That honor was apparently left to Henry L. and Frank McClintock whose report in the May 1958 *Trail and Timberline* indicates that they climbed Purgatory Point some time prior to 1958.

During their July 1932 trip in which they climbed The Hand and the northwest couloir on Mount Sneffels, Williams, Griffiths, and Lavender also made probable first ascents of Kismet by its east ridge and Cirque Mountain by its west ridge. They also made the second ascent of Teakettle Mountain and reported that it "has by far the finest summit of any of the San Juan peaks that we have visited; it is small, solid and well isolated and one can pleasantly perch on its flat surface with the fine sense of segregation from the rest of the world."[10] Williams, Griffiths, and Lavender did not find the register left by Rolfe and Hartman and therefore initially claimed a first ascent of Teakettle.

During the summer of 1933, the San Juan Mountaineers established numerous survey stations. In the process, they made first ascents of Gilpin Peak, Wolcott Peak, Reconnoiter Peak, Peak T O, and Peak S2.

The climbers on the 1934 CMC outing did not limit themselves just to the pinnacles on Mount Sneffels. In addition, they made several notable ascents of high peaks in the area. Don McBride and Everett Long reached the summit of Dallas Peak after "extremely careful and delicate climbing" which at one point involved a shoulder stand.[11] After climbing T O, which was first climbed in July 1933 by Griffiths, A.C. Bartlett and Robert Blair traversed the east ridge of West Dallas Peak to make its first ascent.

After the intensive activity of the early 1930s it seemed as if there was not much to do in the area. Virtually all of the first ascents were taken up by the San Juan Mountaineers' burst of activity. Over twenty years passed before there were reports of new routes in the area. In 1958, David Lewis and Frank McClintock climbed the difficult northwest ridge of Mount Sneffels which was, as far as they knew, "the only major ridge or face route upon the peak that had not yet been climbed."[12]

Interest was renewed in Dallas Peak in 1976 when Spencer Swanger made a solo climb of the peak, which was the last of the hundred highest peaks in Colorado which he had not climbed. Swanger felt that of the nearly 300 climbs he had made, "perhaps

. . . this had been the toughest."[13] Swanger had reviewed the *SJM Guide* which was written prior to McBride and Long's ascent of Dallas in 1934. Since he did not find either a cairn or register on the peak, Swanger incorrectly speculated that he had made a first ascent. In fact, his ascent was probably a third ascent. Stuart Krebs also made a solo climb of Dallas in July 1956.

The first winter ascent of Sneffels was accomplished in February 1934 by Mel Griffiths and Gordon Williams. They approached Sneffels from Blaine Basin, climbed up Scree Col, and then the couloir on the southeast face to the summit. After the trip, Griffiths and Williams triumphantly reported that "Winter mountaineering, the sport, has begun in the San Juans."[14]

In January 1983, the north face of Sneffels was climbed in the winter by Kitty Calhoun and Lyle Dean. Calhoun and Dean climbed the "eastern couloir of the north face for 100 feet and traversed on to the main face," which they then climbed directly to the summit. They reported that the climbing "varied from excellent sixty degree snow to several mixed rock pitches. One open bivouac was made about halfway up the face."[15]

Notes

1. Rhoda, *Summits to Reach*, p. 75.
2. *SJM Guide*, Climbing Notes, p. a.
3. *T&T*, December 1931.
4. *Ibid.*
5. *A.A.J.*, 1933, p. 101.
6. *T&T*, January 1941.
7. *A.A.J.*, 1933, p. 97.
8. *Ibid.*
9. *T&T*, February 1934.
10. *A.A.J.*, 1933, p. 101.
11. *T&T*, October 1934.
12. *T&T*, May 1958.
13. *T&T*, September 1976.
14. *T&T*, March 1934.
15. *A.A.J.*, 1984, p. 191.

ACCESS AND HIKING

Yankee Boy Basin

Yankee Boy Basin is the most popular point of access to the Sneffels Range. To reach the basin, turn west off U.S. 550 just south of Ouray, on a well-maintained gravel road. After leaving U.S. 550, the road heads up spectacular Canyon Creek toward Camp Bird. As you near Camp Bird, the road narrows, as it is carved out of the cliff on the west side of the drainage. When you reach the Camp Bird turnoff at 4.9 miles, stay right and follow the road as it travels past the old town of Sneffels. At one point shortly after the Camp Bird turnoff, the road was actually dug into the side of the cliff with part of the cliff overhanging the road. After 7.1 miles, the road turns to the right into a four-wheel drive road as it climbs toward the upper basin. With four-wheel drive you can continue for a total of 8.7 miles to an elevation of 11,800 feet which is the start of a trail that leads to Blue Lakes Pass. The trail starts at the beginning of the sharp switchback to the right. Some vehicles may be able to make this sharp switchback and the several more which follow to reach the high bench at 12,200 feet.

The trail which starts at the first high switchback traverses the steep slope on the north side of Sneffels Creek to a small lake and old mining cabin at 12,200 feet. From the lake and cabin it heads northwest up to Blue Lakes Pass. If your objective is to climb Sneffels from Yankee Boy Basin, another alternative is to gain the high 12,200-foot bench at the foot of Kismet and head west below the base of Kismet. From most points in Yankee Boy Basin, Mount Sneffels is not visible. The prominent peak to the north of Yankee Boy Basin is actually the eastern shoulder of Kismet. Yankee Boy Basin is connected to Blue Lakes Basin by 12,980-foot Blue Lakes Pass. Dike Col (13,060 feet) between Kismet and Cirque Mountain and Scree Col (13,500 feet) between Mount Sneffels and Kismet connect Yankee Boy Basin with Blaine Basin.

Yankee Boy Basin is the best means of access for climbing Sneffels by the southeast couloir and southwest ridge, Kismet, Cirque, Teakettle, Potosi, and Gilpin.

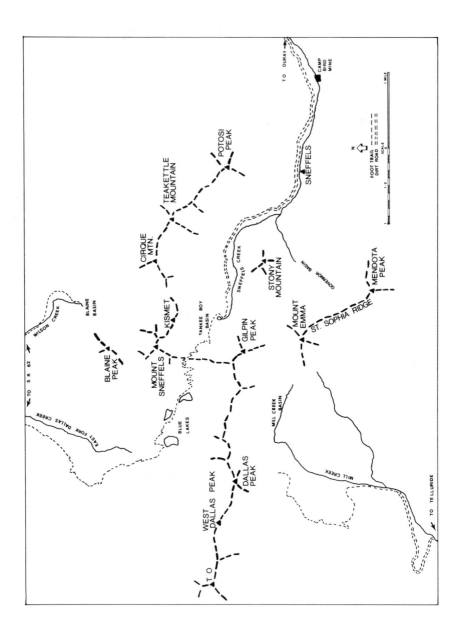

Governor Basin

The initial access for Governor Basin is the same as that for Yankee Boy Basin. After driving past Camp Bird on Road 361 up Canyon Creek, continue for a total of 7.1 miles where the four-wheel drive road takes off to the right for Yankee Boy Basin. Rather than taking a right, continue straight ahead on the four-wheel drive road on the right side of Sneffels Creek. At mile 7.4, you will turn left (south) and cross over Sneffels Creek where you head southwest until you take a left at a junction crossing over to the east side of Governor Basin and switchback your way up to the upper basin. Governor Basin provides the best means of access for Mendota Peak, St. Sophia Ridge, and Mount Emma.

Blaine Basin

The initial turnoff to Blaine Basin is located five miles west of U.S. 550 on Colorado 62. After leaving Colorado 62, take a right at 2.1 miles and continue for a total of 9.2 miles until you reach the Blue Lakes trailhead. The best approach for Blaine Basin follows the Blue Lakes trail for a hundred yards or so before angling off to the left (east) on an abandoned road and crossing the stream on what is left of an old bridge. After crossing the stream, the trail gains a little bit of elevation and contours to meet Wilson Creek. Cross over Wilson Creek and follow the trail on the north for one-half mile before it crosses the stream again. Stay on the south side for another one-half mile before switching back to the north for good. There are a total of three stream crossings. Depending on the time of year, it may be necessary to wade the stream at one or two of the crossings. Most of the elevation is gained over the last mile. The total distance is about two and one-half miles with a gain of 1,400 vertical feet. There are several good camping spots in the flats of the basin. Both the Forest Service and USGS maps show a road which leaves the main road about seven miles from Colorado 62 and angles up to reach Wilson Creek. Although this road used to provide more direct access, it is now closed by a locked gate. Blaine Basin provides an excellent campsite for those interested in the north face of Mount Sneffels or the northeast couloir of Kismet. It is also

possible to climb Cirque from Dike Col or the standard route on
Sneffels from Scree Col. Dike Col is much steeper when
approached from Blaine Basin.

Blue Lakes Trail

The initial access to Blue Lakes Trail is the same as that for
Blaine Basin. After turning right at 2.1 miles, you reach the
trailhead 9.2 miles from Colorado 62. Lower Blue Lake is 3.5 miles
and 1,600 vertical feet from the trailhead. From the lakes the trail
continues up to Blue Lakes Pass and Yankee Boy Basin. The basin
provides access to Dallas Peak, Gilpin Peak, T-O, West Dallas
Peak, and the southwest ridge of Sneffels.

Mill Creek

Mill Creek is probably the best means of access for climbing
Dallas Peak. The route description which follows is based in large
part on an October 1984 *Trail and Timberline* article written by
Bob and Kent Beverly. Just west of the old townsite of San Miguel
and 1.3 miles west of Telluride, turn north (off of Colorado 145)
onto USFS Road No. 637 (Uncompahgre Forest Service Map).
Drive 1.8 miles up Mill Creek to the site of a Telluride
waterworks, beyond which point vehicles are not allowed. Park
here at an elevation of 9,400 feet. Continue up USFS Trail No. 418
from the west (left) side of Mill Creek. The trail crosses a divide
between Mill Creek and Eider Creek at an elevation of 10,600
feet and approximately 1.5 miles from the trailhead. Leave the
USFS trail at this point and continue up the ridge, following an
indistinct but traceable old mining and game trail. On this trail,
climb to an elevation above the Mill Creek band of cliffs. At
about 11,400 feet, it continues to the right, through the last rows
of spruce near timberline, crosses a valley draining the
southwest flank of Dallas, and heads for Mill Creek Basin. As one
rounds the south ridge of Dallas, near timberline, Mill Creek
Basin comes into sight and the trail fizzles out. This point is three
miles from the trailhead. At this point you are on the mountain
itself and ready to start climbing in earnest.

CLIMBING ROUTES

Mount Sneffels (14,150 feet)

SOUTHEAST COULOIR — The southeast couloir is the standard route on Mount Sneffels. The best approach to this route is from Yankee Boy Basin. From most points in Yankee Boy Basin the summit of Mount Sneffels is not visible. What appears to be Sneffels is actually the eastern shoulder of Kismet. Once high in Yankee Boy Basin, contour below the base of Kismet over large talus and boulders until Scree Col between Mount Sneffels and Kismet comes into view. Hike directly up to Scree Col, which you will find to be well-named. From Scree Col, the large prominent southeast couloir lies to the northwest. The couloir is filled with large boulders and, until late in the year, a large

Mount Sneffels as viewed from the summit of Kismet in early July 1985. The standard route follows the snow-filled couloir. *Photo by Robert F. Rosebrough.*

Hal Brown downclimbing Mount Sneffels during a spring snowstorm. Kismet in the background. *Photo by Ernie Stromeyer.*

snowbank. Near the top of the couloir, exit to the left by a narrow slot in the wall. The summit is only a short scramble from the exit to the couloir.

From Scree Col, it is also possible to climb to the left of the couloir out onto the southeast face and follow a steep but well-broken route which generally parallels the couloir. The route on the southeast face is clear of snow much earlier in the year than the couloir.

SOUTHWEST RIDGE — From Yankee Boy Basin, the southwest ridge looks impossible because of the jagged pinnacles just north of Blue Lakes Pass. Actually, the pinnacles are easily passed to the west. From Blue Lakes Pass, two saddles on the ridge are visible—a higher U-shaped saddle (west) and a lower V-shaped saddle (east). Head for the lower V-shaped saddle, but as you near it, traverse left and then climb to the higher saddle. From the higher saddle, you traverse across the top of the steep couloir to the west and then downclimb about fifty yards to a gully which then climbs up to the prominent notch on the southwest ridge at about 13,500 feet. After attaining the top of the notch, climb a south-facing gully to gain the ridge. Once on the ridge, stay directly on the ridge or just to the east. In spots, there is a great deal of exposure to the west. In the spring and early summer, it is possible to gain the ridge by cramponing up to the notch from the east.

NORTH FACE — All of the north face routes are technical. Take a rope and protection. The east couloir route is about half rock and half snow and ice. The northwest couloir is all snow and ice except for the last one hundred feet. The direct route is approached on snow but is primarily rock.

(a) East Couloir and Northeast Arete — This was the first route climbed on the north face of Sneffels. Take the left (east) couloir on the north face. High on the east couloir, take the right branch which ends at the base of a "vertical chimney guarded by a chockstone." The chimney is attacked by ascending "the ice-polished cliff to the left." At the top of the couloir, the route joins the northeast ridge which is followed to the summit. The December 1931 *Trail and Timberline* contains a description and illustration of the route.

(b) Northwest Couloir — The northwest couloir is the couloir on the right (west) side of the north face. The couloir meets another couloir coming down from the summit which is hidden when viewed from below. The route is all snow and ice until 100 feet below the summit. The steepest portion of the couloir (45 to 50 degrees) is the 200 feet just below the junction of the two couloirs. Crampons and a couple of ice tools are essential. The route gets progressively more difficult over the course of the season as the snow turns to water ice.

(c) Direct Route — The direct route on Mount Sneffels follows the cliffs which run down the center of the face. After climbing up the snowfield to the central cliffs, the route stays on rock to the summit. Most of the difficulties are found low on the face. A description and illustration of the route can be found in the

Ike Weaver and Ernie Stromeyer climbing the northwest couloir of Mount Sneffels. *Photo by Robert F. Rosebrough.*

January 1941 *Trail and Timberline.*

NORTHWEST RIDGE — An article in the May 1958 *Trail and Timberline* describes a route on the northwest ridge of Sneffels. Although there is "somewhat rotten rock lower down," the report notes that "there are lots of challenging gendarmes and the climbing above the notch [400 or 500 feet below the top] is on solid rock with a fine view. The variety of couloirs and pinnacles lower down makes route finding interesting, so that one could make quite a number of different climbs before really knowing that side of the mountain." The northwest ridge is a fifth class route. The first ascent party used twelve pitons for protection.

Peak 13,694 "Kismet" (½ mile southeast of Mount Sneffels)

EAST RIDGE — The initial objective on this route is Dike Col (13,060 feet) between Kismet and Cirque. From Yankee Boy Basin, the climb up to Dike Col is easy. From Blaine Basin, it is steep and covered by a large snowbank. The summit of Kismet can't be seen from most points in Yankee Boy Basin. The false summit you see is the east shoulder of the peak. From Dike Col the ridge gets progressively harder. The upper portion of the ridge requires you to scramble third class over loose rock.

NORTH COULOIR — The prominent couloir east of the summit on the north face is a good snow and ice climb. The average angle of the couloir is about forty degrees. Crampons and ice tools are essential. At the top of the couloir you join the upper portion of the east ridge.

Cirque Mountain (13,686 feet)

SOUTHWEST RIDGE — From Dike Col the summit of Cirque is one of the few walkups in the area. Point 13,500 is bypassed to the left (north). You will encounter a very short section of scrambling at 13,400 feet, just below the summit. The register is on the western summit.

Teakettle Mountain (13,819 feet)

SOUTH COULOIR — The point of reference for sorting out the routes on Teakettle is the large basin south of the summit which is bounded on the left (west) by the jutting southwest ridge and on the right (east) by the more rounded southeast face. Just to the right of the southwest ridge is the steep south couloir. Climb directly up the couloir, hugging the left side of the wall. A hard hat is essential for this route as it is not unusual to encounter rockfall from above. Near the top of the couloir, exit to the right and gain the southeast ridge which is composed of loose volcanic scree. The southeast ridge leads to the summit pinnacle which is solid. The summit pinnacle is climbed by a vertical chimney on the east side. Most climbers will want a rope belay on this last pitch. The summit is flat, airy, and surprisingly roomy.

SOUTHEAST COULOIR — Once in the large south basin, climb up the steep talus slope to the right of the basin. It is better to stay in the middle, or to the right, of the talus slope. Most of

Teakettle (left), Little Coffeepot, and Potosi from the eastern shoulder of Kismet. Can you pick out the spout and handle on Teakettle? *Photo by Robert F. Rosebrough.*

the rockfall is encountered on the left side of the talus slope. Once high on the talus slope, you will see a couloir to the left which will lead you to Teakettle's southeast ridge. The rock in the couloir is incredibly loose. The route should not be attempted by large parties or climbers without hard hats. The southeast ridge will lead you to the summit pinnacle.

SOUTHEAST FACE — Although more indirect than the routes described above, this route has less danger of rockfall. Traverse to the right of the south basin and climb up the southeast face of Teakettle directly below the "Little Coffeepot" which is the 13,568-foot point located on the ridge between Teakettle and Potosi. Once at the base of the Little Coffeepot, follow the southeast ridge to the summit pinnacle of Teakettle.

Climbing the final chimney of Teakettle, 1957. *Photo by John Filsinger.*

Little Coffeepot (13,568 feet)

Little Coffeepot is the unofficial name for the block aiguille located between Teakettle and Potosi, which the San Juan Mountaineers referred to as S1. The initial approach is described under the southeast face route for Teakettle. George Bell, Jr. reports that Little Coffeepot can be climbed by any of a number of chimneys on the east side. "Each is about ten vertical feet and very rotten but no harder than the chimney at the top of Teakettle."

Potosi Peak (13,786 feet)

SOUTHEAST FACE — The point of beginning for the southeast face is located on the Yankee Boy Basin Road, 6.2 miles from U.S. 550 at the point where the Imogene Pass Road turns off to the left. The southeast face starts out as a steep climb over grassy slopes which give way to loose talus fields. From below, what appears to be the summit is not. The true summit is several hundred vertical feet above the false summit which you see. Once you pass the false summit and gain the base of the true summit block, contour right (east) to the east face. In contrast to the vertical cliffs which surround the other side of the summit block, the east face is an enjoyable scramble.

SOUTHWEST FACE — The southwest face route starts about 700 vertical feet higher than the southeast face route. It is less direct, however, and involves a contour around the peak to gain the east face.

To begin the route, hike or drive up the Yankee Boy Basin Road for about a mile after it turns to four-wheel drive and park where the road makes a turn to the left as it crosses a stream. From this point climb up the rust-colored talus slope and then begin the contour around Potosi to the east. If you choose this route, make sure you take a good look around when you top out on the first couloir after climbing the rust-colored talus slope. On your return, you need to be sure that you return by the same route. Several of the other couloirs on the lower portion of the southwest face can be very difficult.

Mendota Peak (13,275 feet)

NORTH FACE AND EAST RIDGE — Mendota Peak is located at the southeast end of St. Sophia Ridge. After hiking or driving up the road into Governor Basin, climb into the basin northeast of the peak. From the basin you will see a twin point at 13,220 foot elevation. Climb the western summit and then follow Mendota's east ridge to the summit. Remember that Mendota is the high point extending from St. Sophia Ridge so as not to be confused by the rounded points (Peaks 13,337 and 13,436) located to the east which are actually higher.

Mount Emma (13,581 feet)

EAST FACE — From Governor Basin, climb northwest to gain the east face which is composed of loose scree and talus. The last 100 to 150 feet require some bouldering. There are several variations which will go on this last section.

Gilpin Peak (13,694 feet)

NORTHWEST RIDGE — From Upper Yankee Boy Basin leave the Blue Lakes Trail and aim for the low point on the ridge which separates Blue Lakes Basin from Yankee Boy Basin. Early in the summer, it is possible to crampon up the forty-degree snowfield just east of the ridge to gain the upper ridge. Obstacles on the ridge are generally bypassed to the left (east). Once the upper portion of the ridge is gained, it is a walkup to the summit.

SOUTHEAST RIDGE — From the end of the Yankee Boy Basin road, head southwest to gain the ridge. The lower and middle portions of the ridge are both rough and loose and, in at least one spot, exposed. Some climbers may want a rope belay in spots. The upper portion of the ridge is a walkup.

Dallas Peak (13,809 feet)

SOUTHEAST FACE — From Mill Creek Basin, climb up to the middle section of the southeast face between the prominent couloir on the left (west) and the right (east) side of the face. Climb directly up the face angling to the left. After topping out above the couloirs to your left, traverse below the northeast ridge and angle up toward the summit block. From below, you will see two prominent summit blocks. The north summit block appears higher and is actually the true summit. What you see is not a false summit. Although the southeast face itself involves a fair amount of scrambling, the real difficulties do not begin until the last 200 feet. The first objective is to gain the ledges on the north side of the peak, below the summit block. At the base of the summit block you will find a small snowbank which is the highest snowbank on the southeast face. To the right of the snowbank, between two blocks, is a short couloir which is the best way to gain the ledges. At least one move in the short

Ernie Stromeyer glissading the snowbank just below the summit block on Dallas Peak. *Photo by Robert F. Rosebrough.*

couloir is strenuous and if you have a rope, you might as well break it out at that point. It is also possible to crampon up the snowbank which appears to deadend under some large boulders. In fact there is an exit to the right from the top of the snowbank which is hidden from view when seen from below. Either variation will lead you to the ledges on the north face of the summit block, which you should follow about fifty to seventy-five feet to a crack system which takes you directly to the summit. The ledges leading to the crack system are not particularly difficult. They are broken up and wide enough that you do not feel the full extent of the exposure on the north face. The last 100 feet of the crack system is lower fifth class climbing.

Although several climbers have free climbed Dallas Peak, even good climbers would be well advised to carry a rope and protection for this last section. Knifeblade pitons and small angle pitons seem to work particularly well. Once on the summit, you can either downclimb or rappel the ascent route.

In the October 1984 *Trail and Timberline*, Kent Beverly reported a different route on the lower portion of the southeast face. Beverly started up the southeast face on the far left (west) portion of the face and "traversed across ledges to the main gullies that run down the southeast face of the peak."

BLUE LAKES APPROACH — From the west side of the lower Blue Lake, Rich Reifenberg suggests climbing south and slightly east up a wide gully to the 12,974 saddle on the ridge extending east from Dallas. The gully is steep, loose, and rotten. Once on the ridge, follow it up and over the 13,180 and 13,420 humps until you reach the final summit block. The route on the summit block is the same one described under the southeast face route.

Peak 13,735, "T-O"
(½ mile NE of Campbell Peak)

EAST RIDGE — George Bell Jr. reports that T-O can be "climbed by gaining its east ridge from the high basin above the Blue Lakes."

Peak 13,741, "West Dallas Peak"
(½ mile west of Dallas Peak)

WEST RIDGE — From T-O, Bell climbed West Dallas Peak by the "tedious crumbling ridge between them."

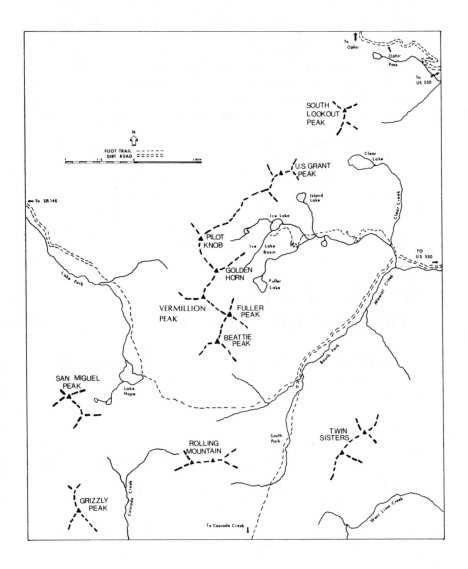

To Ophir

Ophir Pass

To US 550

SOUTH LOOKOUT PEAK

N

FOOT TRAIL
DIRT ROAD

1   1-2   0   1 MILE

Clear Lake

U.S. GRANT PEAK

Island Lake

Clear Creek

To SR 145

Ice Lake

PILOT KNOB

Ice Lake Basin

Fuller Lake

TO US 550

GOLDEN HORN

Lake Fork

Mineral Creek

VERMILLION PEAK

FULLER PEAK

BEATTIE PEAK

South Fork

SAN MIGUEL PEAK

Lake Hope

TWIN SISTERS

South Park

ROLLING MOUNTAIN

GRIZZLY PEAK

Cascade Creek

West Lime Creek

To Cascade Creek

SILVERTON WEST GROUP

This group of seemingly endless peaks is located west and south of Silverton and east and south of Trout Lake and Ophir. To the west, the group is bounded by Colorado 145 between Rico and Ophir and to the east by U.S. 550 from Coal Bank Pass north through Silverton to Red Mountain Pass. Although there are no 14,000-foot peaks in this group, there are many high, rugged, thirteeners. Nine of the 200 highest peaks in Colorado are located within this group.

Vermillion Peak (13,894 feet) is the highest. It is clustered around Ice Lake Basin with Fuller Peak, Golden Horn, Pilot Knob, and U.S. Grant Peak. Pilot Knob is one of the most difficult major mountains in Colorado to climb. The summit of Pilot Knob is formed by a long, narrow ridge with near vertical 200-foot cliffs on all sides. Three or four miles to the southwest of the Ice Lake Basin peaks lie San Miguel Peak, Grizzly Peak, and Rolling Mountain. Although these three high peaks are located within two miles of each other, they are best approached from three separate directions. Northeast of the Ice Lake Basin peaks lie South Lookout Peak and Lookout Peak which straddle Ophir Pass. On the eastern edge of the group are several lower peaks of interest: Engineer Mountain, Jura Knob, Grand Turk, and Sultan Mountain.

CLIMBING HISTORY

The first survey climb made in the San Juans was a climb of Engineer Mountain in late June 1873 by H.G. Prout who was topographic assistant with a U.S. Army Corps of Engineers party led by Lieutenant E.H. Ruffner.

Prout climbed the northeast ridge of Engineer and must have been impressed by the difficulty and exposure since he reported that "the feelings of a solitary man toiling on hands and knees up this edge are not cheerful."[1] Prout was also impressed by the view of the San Juans from Engineer's summit. He doubted that "any other mountain region in the world displays so extensive a mass of such increasing variety of form and so wholly grand."[2]

The following year, a Hayden Survey team led by A.D. Wilson also climbed the northeast ridge of Engineer and "found the ascent of the peak not very tiresome, but rather dangerous."[3] The Hayden party also made the first reported ascents of Vermillion Peak and Sultan Mountain. They reported that the

A.D. Wilson (standing) and Franklin Rhoda on the summit of Sultan Mountain, 1874. *Photo by W.H. Jackson, courtesy of USGS.*

Hayden Survey photographer on the summit of Sultan Mountain, 1874. *Photo by W.H. Jackson, courtesy of USGS.*

top of Vermillion Peak was so small that when the "tripod was set up, we could not pass around it, but had to crawl under it."[4]

The next reported climb in the area was the 1908 climb of Vermillion by William S. Cooper and John Hubbard. Cooper and Hubbard approached Vermillion from Ice Lake Basin and attempted the ridge connecting Vermillion to Golden Horn. A twenty-foot ledge high on the ridge forced Hubbard to "cut foot-holds with his pocket knife" in a "sixty degree snowbank frozen solid" which led to a break in the ledge.[5] Ice axes had not been introduced in Colorado as of 1908. Cooper learned to climb under the guidance of Enos Mills who used a hatchet to cut steps on Longs Peak.

The early 1930s saw numerous first ascents. In August 1931, T.T. Ranney and Jess Wood of the U.S. Geological Survey made the difficult climb of South Lookout Peak.[6] The *SJM Guide*, which was written in 1932, reported that Charles Chase made the first ascent of Pilot Knob "some number of years ago" but neither the exact date nor any details about the climb are known.[7]

In the early 1930s, the Silverton West Group was another area which was explored by the San Juan Mountaineers. In 1931, Dwight Lavender, David Lavender, and Forrest Greenfield approached Vermillion Peak from Trout Lake and reported difficult climbing on the cliffs and couloirs of the south face.[8]

In 1932, the Colorado Mountain Club held its annual summer outing at Ice Lake Basin. During the outing, first ascents were made of U.S. Grant Peak and the western summit of Rolling Mountain. On the climb of U.S. Grant Peak, the party of eight led by Mike Walters reported climbing "a fairly difficult little cliff and skirting along a ledge to the south face."[9] Second ascents were also made of Pilot Knob and South Lookout Peak. On Pilot Knob, Dwight Lavender led a party of five which rounded the summit ridge to the west, after not finding a route on either the east or north side, and climbed the first chimney that they encountered on the west that looked possible.[10] Once on top, they were "somewhat put out to discover" that there was an easier route up the east face to the middle summit from which the true summit to the north could be reached.

Shortly before the 1932 Ice Lake Basin outing, four students from the Michigan School of Mines, Robert Jones, Jerome S. Baer, K. Spencer, and Charles Speer, made what was probably a first ascent of Golden Horn by the south face.

Notes

1. Ruffner, *Reconnaissance in the Ute Country*, p. 24.
2. *Ibid.*
3. Rhoda, *Summits to Reach*, p. 65.
4. William S. Cooper, Unpublished Manuscript entitled "Mountains," p. 77.
5. *Ibid.*, p. 64.
6. *SJM Guide*, p. 95.
7. *Ibid.*, p. 91.
8. *T&T*, September 1931.
9. *T&T*, October 1932.
10. *Ibid.*

ACCESS AND HIKING

Ice Lake Basin

In order to reach Ice Lake Basin, the initial objective is South Mineral Campground. Two miles west of Silverton on U.S. 550, turn left and drive 4.5 miles on a well-maintained gravel road to South Mineral Campground. Where the entrance to the campground turns off to the left, turn right and park on the right side of the road. The trail to Ice Lake Basin starts about 100 yards further up the road and angles up the hillside to the right

Golden Horn from Upper Ice Lake Basin. Vermillion Peak at left. *Photo by Robert F. Rosebrough.*

Ice Lake Basin as viewed from Peak 13,309. Fuller Peak (left), Vermillion Peak, Golden Horn, and Pilot Knob. *Photo by Robert F. Rosebrough.*

(northeast). The trail starts at 9,800 feet. Two miles of steep hiking will bring you to Lower Ice Lake Basin at 11,500 feet. Lower Ice Lake Basin affords the last wooded campsites. After another mile and 750 vertical feet you reach Ice Lake at 12,257 feet. The named peaks rimming Ice Lake Basin from south to north are Fuller Peak, Vermillion Peak, Golden Horn, Pilot Knob, and U.S. Grant Peak. The view of these peaks from upper Ice Lake Basin can be deceiving. From many parts of the basin, Golden Horn is partially obscured by point 13,230. Vermillion is also hard to pick out. Because it is further away, it appears to be shorter than both Golden Horn and Fuller Peak when, in fact, it is over 100 feet higher.

South Park

South Park is located between Rolling Mountain and Twin Sisters. To reach South Park follow the four-wheel drive road which continues past South Mineral Campground. Two miles past the campground, turn left at Bandora Mine and descend to cross the stream. The trail to South Park starts .3 mile after crossing the stream at about 10,700 feet and heads through timber before reaching South Park. From the trailhead, the trail climbs 2.7 miles to an elevation of 12,600 feet. From the top, the trail skirts points 12,766 and 12,703 to the west and follows the ridge between Cascade Creek and Engine Creek down to the bottom of Cascade Creek. From South Park, Rolling Mountain rises to the right (west) and Twin Sisters to the left (east).

Clear Lake Road

The turnoff to Clear Lake is located 3.8 miles from U.S. 550 on the South Mineral Campground road. A well-maintained four-wheel drive road takes you up to the lake at an elevation of 11,940 feet. South Lookout Peak and U.S. Grant Peak can each be climbed from Clear Lake as well as several unnamed peaks which rim the basin. Although you start out high, the routes for South Lookout Peak and U.S. Grant Peak both involve losing and then regaining elevation.

Trout Lake Road — Lake Hope Trail

The road from Trout Lake and the Lake Hope trail provide access from the west for Pilot Knob, Golden Horn, and Vermillion Peak. The Lake Hope trail also provides the most direct route for San Miguel Peak. To reach the Lake Hope trailhead take the turnoff to Trout Lake which is three miles south of the Ophir turnoff on Colorado 145 or fifteen miles northeast of Rico. After turning off 145, skirt Trout Lake to the northeast. Take a sharp turn to the left at 1.8 miles on Hidden Lakes Road, which takes you 2.7 miles to the trailhead. Hidden Lakes Road goes further toward Lake Hope than is indicated on the topo map. The Lake Hope trail starts at about 10,300 feet a couple of hundred yards west of Poverty Gulch.

If you are interested in Pilot Knob or Golden Horn, head up Poverty Gulch. The western ridge of Vermillion is gained just after crossing the creek in Poverty Gulch. If you are interested in San Miguel Peak or Beattie Peak, continue up the Lake Hope trail almost to the lake and then head east for Beattie or west for San Miguel. From the trailhead, it is two miles and 1,600 vertical feet to Lake Hope. Another one-half mile and 600 vertical feet bring you to the 12,445-foot pass overlooking the South Mineral Creek drainage.

From the Lake Hope trailhead, the road continues up to an unnamed lake at 11,200 feet in Groundhog Gulch. This road enters private property, but if not posted for trespassing or locked, provides a higher point of beginning for the west face of Pilot Knob.

Ophir Pass

A four-wheel drive road over Ophir Pass connects Colorado 145 with U.S. 550. The turnoff on 145 is located at the Ophir Loop 7.5 miles south of the Telluride turnoff or eighteen miles northeast of Rico. From the 145 turnoff, the road continues two miles to Ophir and then a total of six miles to the top of the pass at 11,789 feet. The turnoff on U.S. 550 is located five miles northeast of Silverton or 5.2 miles south of Red Mountain Pass. From the 550 turnoff, 4.4 miles will bring you to the top of the pass. The Ophir Pass road provides access to Lookout Peak to the north and South Lookout Peak to the south. The best place to start for Lookout Peak is .2 mile east of the pass. For South Lookout, park at the switchback 1.2 miles east of the pass or 3.2 miles west of 550 and follow the faint trail which contours into Paradise Basin.

Grizzly Peak Road

The best approach for Grizzly Peak is a long dirt road which starts at the old turnoff to the Purgatory Ski Area, which is located twenty-six miles north of Durango or twenty-four miles south of Silverton. When heading north, pass the Purgatory Campground and the main entrance to the Purgatory Ski Area. The turnoff is marked with a sign which says "National Forest

Access, Hermosa Park Road." At .4 mile turn right (north) instead of going on to the ski area and follow a good dirt road which turns sharply to the southwest and winds to the top of the hill. Take the right forks at junctions at 3.4 and 3.8 miles. At the second junction you will see a sign marked "579." Stay on 579 to the end at mile 15.6 after taking a sharp right-hand turn at five miles. The road gets increasingly more difficult with occasional stream crossings and steep places. Passenger cars would probably have a difficult time.

Little Molas Lake

The turnoff to Little Molas Lake is located on U.S. 550, seven miles south of Silverton and forty-three miles north of Durango. This is one mile south of Big Molas Lake and one-half mile north of Molas Pass. From U.S. 550, Little Molas Lake is about one mile from the highway on a well-maintained gravel road. Little Molas Lake makes a good point of beginning for climbs of Grand Turk and Sultan Mountain. The trail which serves as a point of beginning for these climbs starts from the gravel road on the west side of the lake.

CLIMBING ROUTES

Vermillion Peak (13,894 feet)

SOUTHEAST RIDGE — The best way to gain the southeast ridge of Vermillion from Ice Lake Basin is to head for the low point on the ridge between Vermillion Peak and Fuller Peak. Once on the ridge, difficulties are generally avoided by skirting the large blocks on the ridge to the south (left). A couple of spots on the ridge require some scrambling. The final summit consists of very loose rock and care should be taken so as not to dislodge rocks on other members of the climbing party. It is also possible to gain the southeast ridge by a steep couloir about halfway between the summit of Vermillion and the low point on the Fuller-Vermillion Ridge. This couloir is not recommended, however, due to the problems with loose rock.

EAST COULOIR — A steep snow and ice couloir lies directly below the summit to the east. The couloir is best reached by climbing toward the saddle between Golden Horn and Vermillion Peak and then traversing south toward the couloir. Crampons and ice axe are recommended.

Pilot Knob (13,738 feet)

WEST FACE — Pilot Knob has been traditionally approached from Ice Lake Basin to the east. The easiest route, however, on this difficult peak is on the west face which can be approached from the Lake Hope trail and Poverty Gulch or the road on

Pilot Knob from high in Ice Lake Basin. *Photo by Tim Duffy.*

Pilot Knob from the saddle between Pilot Knob and Golden Horn. *Photo by Robert F. Rosebrough.*

private property in Groundhog Gulch. There are two prominent summits on Pilot Knob, the northern summit, which is the highest, and the central summit. In between the main summits are two intermediate summits. The notch between the two intermediate summits is the low point on the summit ridge. The notch can be gained from the west without any technical difficulty. Once on the ridge, the problems begin. You will find a great deal of exposure on both sides. The most difficult spot is the intermediate summit just south of the true (north) summit. Although there is a difficult, exposed traverse to the left (west) which will go, your best bet is simply to go directly over the top. Most people will want a rope belay at this point. A half length rope and three or four knife blade or angle pitons work well. Once over the intermediate summit, the true summit is easy to reach.

EAST FACE COULOIRS — To climb Pilot Knob by either of the east face couloirs, the point of beginning is the saddle between

Ernie Stromeyer at the top of the first "yellow couloir" on the east face of Pilot Knob. *Photo by Robert F. Rosebrough.*

Golden Horn and Pilot Knob which can be reached from either Ice Lake Basin or Poverty Gulch. From the saddle, traverse below the summit block past the central summit. When I climbed Pilot Knob from the east, I climbed the first "yellow couloir" north of the central summit. The lower portion of the couloir was very loose and rotten but not particularly difficult. The last ten or fifteen feet were both rotten and difficult. I would recommend that you protect it. The first couloir tops out at the notch between the central summit and the intermediate summit just to the north. Once on the ridge, follow it directly to the north summit. The two most difficult spots on the ridge are the intermediate summits which are both very exposed and should be protected. As on the west face route, a half length rope and knifeblade and small angle pitons work very well. I would highly recommend a hard hat on both routes. A second "yellow couloir" is described by Garratt and Martin which starts a route which gains the ridge near the low point between the northern and central summits. The Garratt and Martin route is probably better, if for no other reason than that it bypasses the intermediate summit just north of the central summit. When looking for the yellow couloirs be sure to distinguish between a chimney and a couloir. There are a couple of steep yellow chimneys just north of the central summit which should be avoided.

U.S. Grant Peak (13,767 feet)

SOUTHWEST RIDGE — The southwest ridge begins at the 13,220 saddle separating U.S. Grant from Peak 13,520. To reach the saddle leave the Ice Lake Trail in the eastern portion of Lower Ice Lake Basin and climb northwest into the Island Lake Basin and then directly to the saddle. The October 1932 *Trail and Timberline* reports that the first ascent party climbed a "fairly difficult little cliff" and then skirted along a ledge to the south face. From the south face they found the summit was an easy matter.

The crux of U.S. Grant's southeast ridge. *Photo by Tim Duffy.*

Golden Horn (13,780 feet approx.)

SOUTHEAST FACE — From either Ice Lake Basin or Poverty Gulch, climb toward the saddle between Vermillion and Golden Horn. From the saddle, follow the southwest ridge about halfway up before moving out on to the southeast face to the right. There are two summits on Golden Horn. The western, or lefthand summit, is slightly higher. Although Golden Horn looks extremely difficult from most angles, the climb up the southeast face is not hard.

Fuller Peak (13,761 feet)

NORTH FACE — The north face of Fuller Peak is covered by a large snowfield. The snowfield can be climbed directly to gain the ridge between Fuller Peak and Vermillion Peak. Once the ridge is gained, it is an easy walkup to the summit.

NORTHEAST RIDGE — The rock band on the lower portion of the ridge is skirted by going out on to the east face. After reaching the top of the rock band, it is quicker to contour back over to gain the ridge, rather than fighting the loose rock on the east face. Once back on the ridge, the best route climbs just to the right (west). As you near the top, you encounter some scrambling.

Beattie Peak (13,342 feet)

NORTH RIDGE — The north ridge begins at the 13,020-foot saddle connecting Beattie to Fuller Peak. The saddle can be reached from the west by the basin above the Lake Hope trail or from the east by climbing from the four-wheel drive road above South Mineral Campground. Once at the saddle, the summit is only a little over 300 vertical feet above.

South Lookout Peak
(13,380 feet approx.)

EAST FACE — The east face can be reached by contouring into Paradise Basin from the Ophir Pass road or from Clear Lake. If you are coming over from Clear Lake, go north to gain the ridge separating Clear Lake from Paradise Basin before the pinnacles on the western portion of the ridge and then drop down into Paradise Basin. The east face is a maze of rotten couloirs. I have a hard time recommending a route on the east face since I was not pleased with the north-central couloir I chose, but did not see anything better. The highlight of the route for me was a headfirst fall down the steep couloir while glissading on the descent. In any event, if you reach the summit block, the best route follows a left leaning crack on the south face. It is about seventy-five feet high and should be protected. Another route which also involves some lower fifth class climbing is found on the southeast side of the summit block but involves much more loose rock than the south face crack.

SOUTHEAST FACE - SOUTHERN RIDGE — From Clear Lake it is easy to reach the southern summit of South Lookout. To reach the true summit, however, it is necessary to make a difficult, rotten traverse around the false summit just south of the highest summit on the right (east). I wouldn't do it again without a rope and protection.

Lookout Peak (13,661 feet)

SOUTH RIDGE — The best spot to start this climb is .2 mile east of Ophir Pass. This allows you to bypass the rounded hill (12,187 feet) to the east. You can avoid the steep rotten sections on the lower ridge by heading up into the basin southeast of the peak. The south ridge is then gained from the east. There are some steep sections on the ridge with plenty of loose rock.

NORTHEAST RIDGE — The northeast ridge is a series of vertical blocks and pinnacles separating Lookout Peak from Peak 13,614. The northeast ridge is gained best by the rounded ridge

Mark Pirlot climbing Lookout Peak, May 1985. South Lookout Peak in the background. *Photo by Robert F. Rosebrough.*

which runs northeast from Chapman Gulch, a mile and a half west of Ophir Pass. When we climbed Lookout in the spring from this direction, we crossed over the ridge and traversed below it to the east. It was steep and exposed. If I were ever foolish enough to try this route again, I would try to traverse the ridge to the west. I would also take a rope to belay a couple of sections. It is much more difficult to gain the summit from the north than the south.

San Miguel Peak (13,752 feet)

NORTHEAST RIDGE — To reach the northeast ridge, leave the Lake Hope trail before it reaches the lake and traverse toward the lake's outlet. To bypass the large, jutting buttress on the

Approaching San Miguel Peak on snowshoes, Memorial Day, 1985. The skyline is formed by Pilot Knob (left), Golden Horn, Vermillion, Fuller, and Beattie peaks. *Photo by Ernie Stromeyer.*

lower portion of the ridge, gain the ridge from the east at about 12,500 feet. Once on the ridge, follow it directly to the summit.

WEST RIDGE — The west ridge begins at the 13,260 pass separating San Miguel from Peak 13,491. The pass is reached by leaving the Lake Hope trail at about 11,000 elevation and contouring into the drainage to the north of San Miguel. Once on the ridge, bypass the large rock face to the right (south). The final portion of the ridge is a little narrow and exposed in spots.

Rolling Mountain (13,693 feet)

EAST BASIN - SOUTHEAST RIDGE — The approach for this

route starts at the Rico-Silverton trail and follows the trail to South Park. From South Park, climb directly up into the large basin east of Rolling Mountain. In the lower basin, it is best to climb the talus and boulderfield left (south) of the stream, rather than bushwacking through the brush right (north) of the stream. Once in the upper basin, bear to the left (south) to gain the southeast ridge. You are required to do some scrambling over loose rock to gain the ridge. A couple of points on the ridge also require some scrambling before you reach the summit.

SOUTHEAST BASIN - SOUTHWEST FACE — This route is both easier and more roundabout than the east basin route. To gain the southeast basin, follow the Rico-Silverton trail for a half mile after reaching South Park before leaving the trail and heading west. Once at the top of the basin, contour north to gain the southwest face which is composed of loose scree and talus. My preference is to use the east basin route on the ascent and the southeast basin on the way down.

Peak 13,506 "Lake Point"
(½ mile northwest of San Miguel Peak)

EAST FACE — Lake Point is the block-topped peak east of Sheep Mountain which is clearly visible from the Trout Lake area. The best approach leaves the Lake Hope trail to contour into the drainage north of San Miguel Peak. The east face is a steady climb over small loose rock to reach the thirty-foot, near vertical summit block. The summit can be reached either from the east or the west. The route on the east is easier than it looks because of a ledge which is out of view from the bottom. A short rope for a belay on the summit block would be welcome.

Grizzly Peak (13,738 feet)

SOUTH COULOIR - SOUTHWEST FACE — From the end of the Grizzly Peak road, you can see a trail when looking north across the canyon. Begin contouring northwest to cross the stream and gain the trail. The main trail drops down into Cascade Gulch and is to be avoided. Look for a less distinct trail which angles uphill toward timberline. Once you reach timberline, maintain your elevation and head north to the ponds and marshy area at 11,500 or bypass them to the left (west) and begin climbing to the wide couloir or gully on the south face which leads to the southwest ridge and the face. In the couloir you will be climbing on large, steep talus. The southwest face is also strewn with large talus and boulders.

Twin Sisters (13,374 and 13,432 feet)

WEST RIDGE — To reach the west ridge of the southwest sister, leave the Rico-Silverton trail in South Park and climb through oak brush and grassy slopes to reach the rocky talus slope ridge. Haskell Rosebrough reports that the ridge is neither exposed nor particularly difficult. Although the talus is tedious, the views from both summits are very worthwhile. The ridge between the sisters presents no difficulty at all.

Engineer Mountain (12,968 feet)

NORTHEAST RIDGE — The northeast ridge of Engineer Mountain is best approached from Coal Bank Pass. From the top of Coal Bank Pass, the most direct route is to hike northeast to gain the steep bench west of the pass. After gaining the bench, hike one mile west to the base of the northeast ridge. The ridge is bounded to the north by sheer cliffs. To the south, the angle is not as severe. The ridge takes you directly to the summit. A couple of spots require some scrambling.

Jura Knob (12,614 feet)

SOUTHEAST RIDGE — The southeast ridge of Jura Knob which is best reached by the trail up Coal Creek is a long, moderate hike above timberline. Only a short ledge not far from the summit presents any difficulty.

Sultan Mountain (13,368 feet)

SOUTH RIDGE — Sultan Mountain is usually climbed in conjunction with Grand Turk. From the eastern summit of Grand Turk, Haskell Rosebrough reports that you can either stay high on the ridge and downclimb to the 12,776 saddle separating Grand Turk and Sultan or traverse the western summit points to the south and the west to gain the saddle. From the saddle, go straight up the ridge the 592 vertical feet to Sultan's summit. Rather than reclimbing Grand Turk, the best return route to Little Molas Lake is to drop toward the Bear Creek drainage and contour west and then south around peak 12,849 on game trails through the brush to the trail that comes up from Bear Creek and takes you back to Little Molas Lake.

Grand Turk (13,180 feet approx.)

SOUTHWEST RIDGE — The best route for Grand Turk begins on the trail which heads northwest from Little Molas Lake. Haskell Rosebrough suggests turning off the trail to contour north into the basin between unnamed peaks 12,849 and 12,734. From the bowl, contour to the right (east) of peak 12,899 and climb directly up and over the top of peak 13,087. From the top of 13,087, follow the ridge down to the saddle and then traverse right to the eastern summit which affords views of Silverton to the north and Molas Lake and Andrews Lake to the south. Although you will encounter some steep talus, the climb is not particularly difficult.

Peak 13,309, "V 2"
(1/3 miles southwest of Clear Lake)

NORTH FACE - WEST RIDGE — This is an easy but very enjoyable climb. From Clear Lake, climb southwest to gain the 12,860 pass northwest of the flat summit. After gaining the ridge, follow it around to the summit. From the summit you have an excellent view of Ice Lake Basin and the rugged peaks which circle it.

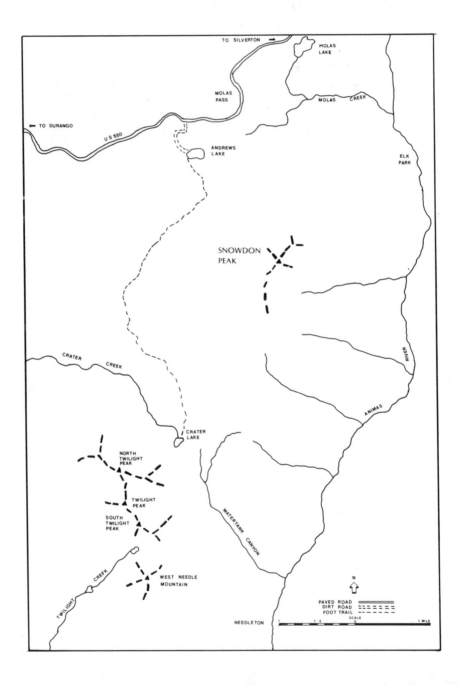

WEST NEEDLE
MOUNTAINS

The West Needle Mountains are a small cluster of peaks separated from the Needles and Grenadiers by the four to five thousand-foot deep gorge created by the Animas River. The group is comprised of Snowdon Peak to the north and North Twilight Peak, Twilight Peak, South Twilight Peak, and West Needle Mountain to the south. A day climb of Snowdon Peak is one of the more delightful climbs in the San Juan Range. Snowdon is easily accessible and offers a choice of exciting routes. The view from the large, roomy summit gives the full panorama of the Needle and Grenadier ranges.

In contrast to Snowdon Peak, the Twilights and West Needle Mountain are more remote and are best climbed in conjunction with an overnight backpack into Crater Lake. All three of the Twilights and West Needle Mountain offer challenging and at times exposed climbing. While the Twilights can be reached after a pleasurable backpack, there is simply no reasonable way to get to West Needle Mountain. Climbing West Needle Mountain from Crater Lake makes for a very long day. The other options are even more unpleasant. The long steep bushwhacks west from Needleton or east from Lime Creek Road would be difficult at best.

CLIMBING HISTORY

The first recorded ascent of Snowdon Peak was made by the Hayden Survey in September 1874. From the top of Snowdon, Rhoda reported that the Hayden team "obtained the most striking view of the quartzite mountains."[1] Rhoda also remarked that the summit of Snowdon was poised "on the brink of the great Animas Canyon, which here is over 4,000 feet in depth; a few miles further down it is still deeper."[2] Snowdon Peak is named for Francis M. Snowden (note different spelling) who built the first cabin in Silverton the same year that the Hayden party made the first ascent of the peak.

Other than the first ascent of Snowdon, reports on climbs in the West Needles are sparse. In the *SJM Guide*, Carleton Long reported that "the West Needle Mountains are, even today, relatively unexplored. There are no recorded ascents of any of the peaks except Snowdon, which was climbed by the Hayden Survey and, while it is possible that most or all of the peaks have been climbed by prospectors or other peregrinating individuals, there still remains for the mountain climber a wealth of unexplored routes."[3]

Notes

1. Rhoda, *Summits to Reach*, p. 85.
2. *Ibid.*
3. *SJM Guide*, p. 131.

ACCESS AND HIKING

Crater Lake Trail

The Crater Lake trail starts at Andrews Lake, near Molas Pass. The turnoff to Andrews Lake is eight miles south of Silverton and forty-two miles north of Durango on U.S. 550. A well-maintained gravel road turns off 550 three-quarters of a mile south of Molas Pass. From 550, it is only one-third of a mile to Andrews Lake and ample parking.

From Andrews Lake the five-mile trail starts at 10,744 feet and ends at an elevation of 11,600 feet. From Andrews Lake the trail climbs a little over 400 vertical feet to the south. After topping out, you lose, regain, and lose again, 200 feet of elevation before slowly gaining elevation to reach Crater Lake. The total distance from Andrews Lake to Crater Lake is five miles. There are several excellent camping spots at Crater Lake.

From Crater Lake, a rounded saddle which overlooks Watertank Canyon and the Animas River lies several hundred yards and 150 vertical feet to the southwest. Don't be tempted to use Watertank Canyon as an access to the Animas River and Needleton. Those who have tried it do not recommend it.

CLIMBING ROUTES

Snowdon Peak (13,077 feet)

NORTHEAST RIDGE — Where the Crater Lake trail briefly tops out one-half mile south of Andrews Lake, leave the trail and head southeast for three-quarters of a mile. From that point, aim to climb east to the 12,340-foot saddle between Snowdon and

Peak 12,628 or Snowdon's northeast ridge south of the saddle. Once on the ridge, follow it directly toward the summit. Near the top it is best to leave the ridge where it narrows at the top of the prominent northwest couloir and contour left across the east face to gain the southeast ridge. The southeast ridge takes you to the summit. The traverse of the east face involves delicate and somewhat exposed climbing.

WEST BUTTRESS — The 800-foot west buttress descends directly from the summit. When viewed head on from U.S. 550, the buttress look overwhelming. In reality, it is a difficult but very enjoyable climb. The lower section of the buttress is a scramble over large broken sections. The climbing becomes more difficult and exposed higher on the buttress. Although many strong parties climb the route third class in good weather, it would be advisable to take a rope and several pieces of protection.

North Twilight Peak (13,075 feet)

EAST RIDGE — From Crater Lake, hike south up to the small lake at 11,750 feet and then southwest to gain the ridge which is then followed to the summit.

SOUTH FACE — After gaining the east ridge, you can contour across the southeast face to the saddle between North Twilight and Twilight. From the saddle, the south face is a walkup to the top.

NORTH COULOIR — From Crater Lake, traverse west across the north face to gain the prominent snow chute. This is a steep climb and care must be taken because of loose rock, particularly late in the year. Because of the problem with loose rock, this route should not be attempted by large parties.

Twilight Peak (13,158 feet)

NORTH RIDGE — The summit is roughly 400 vertical feet above the saddle between North Twilight and Twilight. The

Ike Weaver approaching Snowdon Peak in March 1983. *Photo by Robert F. Rosebrough.*

Snowdon Peak's northeast ridge. Note climber on lower left portion of ridge. *Photo by Robert F. Rosebrough.*

north ridge connecting the saddle and the summit is tricky in a couple of spots and has turned back a novice or two.

South Twilight (13,100 feet approx.)

NORTHWEST RIDGE — When South Twilight is climbed in conjunction with Twilight Peak, downclimb the south ridge of Twilight Peak and from the saddle connecting the two peaks, the summit of South Twilight Peak is only 200 vertical feet above.

EAST FACE — When climbed alone from Crater Lake, climb toward North Twilight Peak's east ridge and then contour around the large basin which drains the eastern flanks of the

Twilight Peaks. Once on the east face of South Twilight Peak, it is a third class scramble up the well-broken face. Those discouraged by the east face can continue the traverse south to gain the southeast ridge which can be followed to the summit.

West Needle Mountain (13,045 feet)

There does not appear to be any easy way to approach or climb West Needle Mountain. The alternatives seem to be bushwacking 4,000 vertical feet from Lime Creek, climbing 4,800 vertical feet from Needleton, or combining West Needle with the Twilights in a very long day from Crater Lake. None is particularly inviting.

The east face of Pigeon Peak. *Photo by George Bell.*

NEEDLE MOUNTAINS

The Needles, together with their northern counterparts the Grenadiers, are the heart of the San Juans. They are truly a mountaineering paradise. After at least a day's backpack, you find yourself in an area with seemingly limitless climbing opportunities.

The most frequently climbed peaks in the Needles are the Chicago Basin fourteeners: Mount Eolus, Sunlight Peak, and Windom Peak. Although Eolus, Sunlight, and Windom are by no means the most difficult fourteeners in Colorado or even the San Juans, they tend to be underestimated. They are by no means walkups.

While the Chicago Basin area tends to be overcrowded at certain times of the year, most of the other areas in the Needles are generally sparsely traveled. It is easy to go a day or two without encountering other parties.

Pigeon Peak and Jagged Mountain are two of Colorado's more challenging centennial peaks. Each requires excellent route finding skills and challenges even experienced mountaineers. A wealth of other high thirteeners, including Animas Mountain, Monitor Peak, Glacier Point, Jupiter Mountain, Turret Peak, and Peaks Fifteen and Thirteen, provide a wide variety of climbing opportunities and challenges.

Technical climbers have been lured into the area by pinnacles

Little Finger (left), Peak 16, Peak 15, and Turret Peak (partially obscured). *Photo by George Bell.*

such as The Index and Gray Needle and the large faces such as Monitor's east face and the north face of North Eolus. There also remains much technical climbing to be done in the area such as Pigeon's east face and the north buttress of Turret.

In short, there is something for everybody in the Needles. It is a place you can look forward to coming back to year after year. It will be a long time before you run out of things to climb.

CLIMBING HISTORY

The Needles are one of the few areas in the San Juans which were not explored by members of either the Hayden or Wheeler surveys. The reports of the early surveyors were, however, filled with descriptions of the "Quartzites" which was the term they used to describe an area encompassing both the Needles and

Grenadiers. In addition to the rugged profile of this range, Rhoda of the Hayden Survey was particularly impressed with the weather pattern in the area:

> Early in the day we noticed clouds hovering about the quartzite peaks, as we had seen them so often before. They never completely veiled all the peaks in the group, but early each day began to circle about them in a restless sort of way, like so many mighty lions about their lair. To us this apparent restlessness suggested a consciousness of their terrific destructive power, which only awaited a mandate from the 'God of Storms' to be set in motion. We even now held these peaks in awe, as there seemed to be established somewhere in their midst a regular 'manufactory of storms'.[1]

Given this description, it is not surprising that the highest peak in the range, Eolus, was given its name in honor of the Greek god of the winds.

Beginning in the late 1870s, Needle Creek and Chicago Basin were invaded by prospectors and miners. The high peaks which rim Chicago Basin, including the three fourteeners in the area, Eolus, Windom, and Sunlight, were all probably climbed during this period by miners.

The first party to be lured into the Needles solely by its climbing possibilities was William S. Cooper and John Hubbard in 1908. A couple of years earlier in 1906, Cooper had visited Silverton and climbed Kendall Mountain. From the summit of Kendall, he saw "mountains that I must see again and at the earliest opportunity; the whole San Juan country, the Needle Mountains in particular, and, first of all, Pigeon Peak."[2]

Cooper and Hubbard approached Pigeon from New York Basin. They were forced to abandon an attempt on the south face, "next to the east facing precipice." A rain shower and "an uncomfortably smooth granite slope leading to a series of two or three steps of giant size" forced them to retreat and try a gully on the south face further west. Two or three hundred feet below the summit, they were forced left (west) from their direct route to a notch on the southwest ridge from which they were able to reach the summit. After sunbathing there for two and a half hours, their "final deed was to look down the 1500-foot [actually 900-foot] 85-degree east face—almost as spectacular as the east face of Longs."[3] Although Cooper kept a private diary of the trip, no report of their exploits was published at that time.

Pigeon was next climbed by two well-known pioneers in Colorado mountaineering history. In 1920, Albert R. Ellingwood and Barton Hoag reached the summit via "the large, prominent crack or couloir running up the south face."[4] This was probably the same route taken by Cooper and Hubbard. Ellingwood and Hoag did not find any evidence of the 1908 ascent and in their reports incorrectly assumed that they had made a first ascent. Ellingwood and Hoag also climbed neighboring Turret Peak and apparently did achieve a first ascent of it.

In 1920 and 1927 the summer outings of the Colorado Mountain Club were held in Chicago Basin. During these outings, mass ascents were made of the Chicago Basin peaks, including Eolus, North Eolus, Sunlight, Windom, Jupiter, and Aztec. In addition, a large party during the 1920 outing made a probable first ascent of Grizzly Peak to the southeast of Chicago Basin.

The 1930s were a period of intense activity in the Needles. More difficult routes were established on the fourteeners and several difficult traverses were made in the Chicago Basin area. In addition, climbers began making ascents of the rugged thirteeners in the area such as Jagged Mountain, Animas Mountain, and Monitor Peak.

The first ascents of Jagged Mountain and several other peaks in the area were made during the 1933 climbing expedition of the San Juan Mountaineers. On their first attempt at climbing Jagged, Dwight Lavender, Mel Griffiths, Lewis Giesecke, H.L. McClintock, and Carleton Long climbed the western or third highest summit. The party reached the third summit in wet weather and did not attempt the difficult traverse over to the highest summit. Two days later, the party returned to the south face of Jagged and climbed a route which started in a gully immediately west of the highest summit. This gully led the party to the summit just west of the true summit. From this intermediate summit, they rappeled down to the col and scrambled up 150 feet to the final summit.[5] In the 1934 *American Alpine Journal*, Lavender reported that "Jagged Mountain is probably the most difficult peak yet ascended in the Colorado Rockies." During the 1933 expedition, the San Juan Mountaineers also climbed both summits of Twin Thumbs, Peak Eleven, Peak Twelve, and Peak Six. All were probably first ascents, except Peak Six, which had been climbed by at least one other party.

A small tram car running across the Animas River near Noname Creek on steel cables in tyrolean traverse fashion during the 1937 outing of the Colorado Mountain Club. *Photo by Louise Roloff.*

The second ascent of Jagged Mountain was made in July of 1934 by William P. House and Elizabeth Woolsey who established a route further east on the south face which climbed to a col near the east end of the main ridge of the mountain and then "traversed along the north faces of the pinnacles until about 150 feet below the true summit."[6] Woolsey reported a "rare fall while leading, when a chockstone rolled over as I tried to pull myself up and over it. Fortunately for me, I landed on Bill's head and he fielded me very neatly."[7] The descent was made down the north face by what is probably now the standard route on Jagged. House and Woolsey also climbed Sunlight Peak's north face, "traversing east to the ridge 100 feet or so below the summit."[8]

Carleton Long, Everett Long, and John Nelson climbed Animas Mountain in July of 1934 by a "hidden gully in the south wall of the peak," which they discovered after "attaining a grassy basin on the south side of the mountain."[9]

During the 1930s, interest was shown in difficult traverses as well as first ascents. Mel Griffiths and Bob Ormes made the first traverse of Needle Ridge between Sunlight and Peak Eleven, in July 1937. The traverse required rappels at several points and "practically every variety of rock technique was called into play."[10] In August 1937, during another Colorado Mountain Club outing in the area, Bob Blair and Prather Ashe traversed the ridge from Jupiter to Windom. Later during the outing, a large party led by Jack Heeney extended the traverse from Jupiter over Windom to Sunlight. The second traverse led by Heeney was accomplished over the course of two days. It was reported that the "traverse of the entire ridge is recommended to those who are interested in rock climbing. It offers work which, while never lacking in interest, is never highly technical."[11]

Frank McClintock rappeling from the summit of Peak 15 after its first ascent in August 1940. *Photo by Joe Merhar.*

The Index is a prominent pinnacle just west of Animas Mountain. In September of 1934, a San Juan Mountaineers party consisting of Griffiths, H.L. McClintock, and Frank McClintock made a reconnaissance of The Index and reported that a ridge leading to the "true summit is wild beyond description."[12] On September 6, 1937, the same party returned to The Index and reached the summit by means of a difficult and complicated route.

During the 1930s, Pigeon Peak received renewed interest. In August of 1935, H.L. McClintock, Frank McClintock, and Lewis Giesecke discovered what is now the standard route on Pigeon. From a camp in Ruby Basin above Ruby Lake, they "walked up" the grassy ledges on the west side of the north face.[13] They made the first traverse of Pigeon by descending the southeast chimney. The descent "offered some spectacular work."[14] Frank and H.L. McClintock returned in 1936 with Mary McClintock and Gordon Williams to make the first ascent of the difficult southeast chimney, which had apparently turned back Cooper and Hubbard in 1908.

During the 1940s, there were not as many new routes established in the area, but several climbs are noteworthy. Frank and H.L. McClintock returned in August 1940 with Joe Merhar and Chris Schoredos and established a new route on Eolus and made three probable first ascents. Their route on the west face of Eolus involved a "tricky traverse across the face from a chimney that proved impassable to an adjoining one which 'went'." The three probable first ascents made by the party were of Peaks Fifteen, Sixteen, and Seventeen (Little Finger) which lie between Eolus and Turret Peak and are more commonly known as the Turret Needles. The most difficult of the Turret Needles to climb was Peak Seventeen. The route established by the party partially ascended a chimney on the south face.[15]

Undoubtedly, the most difficult climb of this era, not only in the San Juans but in all of Colorado, was the August 9 and 10, 1947 ascent of the east face of Monitor Peak by Joseph Stettner, John Speck, and Jack Fralick. Stettner was a climber from Chicago who had previously gained a degree of fame by establishing the difficult Stettner's Ledges route on the east face of Longs Peak with his brother Paul. The route on the 1,200-foot east face of Monitor was accomplished only after the party was forced to bivouac high on the route. In the report of the climb, Joe Stettner is quoted as saying that the climb was "the most difficult climb

Jack Fralick (left) and John Speck at daybreak after a rainy bivouac high on the east face of Monitor Peak. August 10, 1947. *Photo by Joe Stettner.*

Climbing equipment used during the 1947 climb of the east face of Monitor Peak. Cleat Army Bramani boots, Army boots with steel spikes projecting from the sole, piton hammers, pitons, carabiners, 120-foot coil of 7/16-inch nylon climbing rope, and 30-foot length of 5/16-inch manilla sling rope. *Photo by Joe Stettner.*

that I have ever accomplished—even more severe than the north wall of the Grand Teton and the Stettner's Ledges route on the east face of Longs Peak."[16] While in the area, Stettner also made the first west to east traverse of Needle Ridge with Marguerette Sharp, Donald Gruber, and Edmund Lowe.

The only reported climbs of note which took place during the 1950s were made during a joint outing of the American Alpine Club and the Colorado Mountain Club in 1953. During that outing, the first ascent of Gray Needle, at the west end of Jagged Mountain, was made by a party that was forced to use expansion bolts for one thirty-foot stretch of the climb.[17] New routes were also worked out on Sunlight, Twin Thumbs, and Animas.

Interest in the Needles was renewed during the 1960s. In 1960, a party of eight led by Charles Walsmith opened a new route on the northeast corner of Pigeon Peak. The route "ascended the first two small couloirs lying north of the east (or southeast) face of Pigeon which faces Turret and attained the northwest ridge about 200 feet below the summit."[18] Several pitons were used for protection. Rockfall, which was a problem on other routes, was "a very slight hazard even with our large party."[19]

George Bell, David Michael, and John Marshall climbed the summit pinnacle on Sunlight Spire in July 1961 using direct aid to climb "a large vertical crack on the north side of the summit obelisk."[20] During this trip, George Bell and Grant Mathews also climbed what they named "Ominous Pinnacle" which lies in the Noname Creek drainage midway between Animas Mountain and Peak Thirteen.

In September 1968, Joe Stettner's nephew, Paul Stettner, Jr., and Larry Dalke established a more direct route on the east face of Monitor Peak. The 1968 route lies north of the 1947 route and joins the original route high on the face. One section at mid-height on the 1968 route required "continuous direct aid."[21] A line between the 1947 and 1968 routes was established on July 4, 1976 by Gary Neptune, Rob Blair, Melisa Geise, and Tom Norton who summited at 9:00 p.m. and ended a long day by making a moonlight downclimb and rappel into Ruby Basin.[22] Yet another line on the lower two-thirds of the east face was established in July 1980, by Larry Coats, Tim Coats, and Jim Haisley. The 1980 route starts to the right of the 1968 route but converges with the other routes on the upper face.

Several climbs of note were made in the area during the late 1970s. In June 1977, Alan Roberts and Ted Kerasote climbed the sheer northwest spur of Knife Point.[23] The north face of North Eolus was climbed by Tony Meyer and Davis (first name unavailable) in 1978.[24] In 1979 the Chicago Mountaineering Club held an outing in Chicago Basin. Various members of the club established several technical routes on the eastern side of the south face of Peak Eighteen. They also repeated Sunlight Spire using aid but speculated that it "could go as a free lead."[25]

The inaccessibility of the Needles discouraged winter climbing until 1966. In that year, Sunlight and Windom were climbed on December 22 and 23 by Don Monk, Kermith Ross, and Phil Schmuck. This party hiked up the narrow gauge tracks from Rockwood. They reached the old miner's cabin at the Twin Lakes after three days with the assistance of food caches placed earlier in the year. They also made an attempt on Eolus but were turned back high on the peak by "threatening weather and a precarious-looking snowcovered north ridge."[26]

The first winter ascent of Eolus was left for Barry Nash, Rick Nolting, Steve Lewis, and Lloyd Frank who started from the Purgatory Ski Area on U.S. 550 between Durango and Silverton. After their snowshoe approach down Cascade Creek and up the Animas River and Needle Creek, they too reached the miner's cabin after three days. On January 26, 1971, they climbed the north ridge of Eolus. Although being somewhat taken aback by their first view of the summit ridge, they reported that the route was "considerably easier than it had looked" and that the "snow was more of a help than hindrance, for the loose stuff was fairly well cemented together and belays were unnecessary."[27]

Notes

1. Rhoda, *Summits to Reach*, pp. 31-32.

2. William S. Cooper, Unpublished Manuscript entitled "Mountains," p. 31.

3. *Ibid.*, p. 69.

4. Bueler, *Roof of the Rockies*, p. 167.

5. *T&T*, November 1933, pp. 155-157.

6. *T&T*, February 1935, p. 17.

7. Elizabeth D. Woolsey, *Off the Beaten Trail*, p. 45.

8. *T&T*, February 1935, p. 17.

9. *T&T*, February 1935, pp. 16-17.

10. *T&T*, July 1937, p. 80.

11. *T&T*, October 1937, p. 105.

12. *T&T*, February 1935, p. 17.

13. *T&T*, September 1947, p. 145.

14. *American Alpine Journal*, 1936, p. 546.

15. *T&T*, September 1951, pp. 113-114.

16. *T&T*, December 1947, p. 195.

17. *A.A.J.*, 1954, p. 170.

18. *T&T*, October 1960.

19. *Ibid.*

20. *T&T*, February 1962, p. 19.

21. *T&T*, July 1969, pp. 126-127.

22. Personal correspondence, Tom Norton.

23. *T&T*, May 1978.

24. *Climbing*, January-February 1979.

25. *The Chicago Mountaineer*, Spring 1980, p. 36.

26. Borneman and Lampert, *A Climbing Guide to Colorado's Fourteeners*, p. 226.

27. *T&T*, July 1971, p. 149.

ACCESS AND HIKING

Durango & Silverton Narrow Gauge Railroad

The narrow gauge train is the most convenient way to start a trip into the Needles. By taking the train, you save at least nine and a half miles of hiking.

At the time of this writing, the train makes the full trip from Durango to Silverton from May 11 through October 27. During the winter, the train still operates, but goes only to Cascade Canyon, six miles south of Needleton, before stopping and returning to Durango. During the summer, three trains (7:30, 8:30, and 9:30) make the round trip but only the 8:30 train serves backpackers.

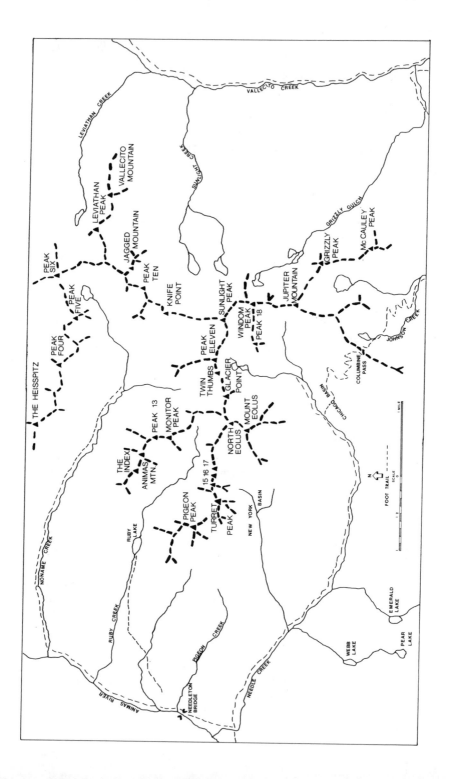

The train makes a regular stop at Needleton (10:44 a.m.) on the way to Silverton. To catch the train on its way back to Durango, you need to flag it down by waving your arms in front of your knees ("like you're doing the Charleston").

Flag the train from the bridge side of the tracks at Needleton and the siding side of the tracks at Elk Park. Backpackers holding return tickets will be boarded first. Any additional space is sold on a first come, first served, basis. On its return, the train passes through Needleton at 2:50 p.m. before reaching Durango at 5:10 p.m. Summer reservations should be made at least a month in advance. The current reservation number is (303) 247-2733. The mailing address is 179 Main Avenue, Durango, Colorado 81301. Tickets must be paid for and picked up in Durango by 6:00 p.m. the day before departure. Pets, firearms, and hunting gear are not permitted on the train.

Over the years, the schedule and policies of the train have changed and will continue to do so. It would be worth your while to confirm times and policies when you make reservations.

Purgatory Creek Trail

The Purgatory Creek Trail provides a means of access to Needleton by foot rather than railroad. The trail starts at the Purgatory Campground located on U.S. 550 twenty-six miles north of Durango or twenty-four miles south of Silverton. Purgatory Campground is located across the highway from the Columbine Ranger Station and the turnoff to the Purgatory Ski Resort. From the campground, the trail steeply descends 1.5 miles through the wooded Purgatory Creek drainage to Purgatory Flats. Once in Purgatory Flats, the trail turns south and follows the Cascade Creek drainage for three miles down to the Animas River. The USGS map incorrectly shows the crossing of Cascade Creek and the Animas River. The old bridge across Cascade Creek has been washed out for several years and the trail now crosses the Animas River over a suspension footbridge. The trail never does cross Cascade Creek. Once across the Animas River, you will be south of the railroad bridge which crosses the Animas. The trail up to Needleton turns off to the right just before the railroad bridge and follows the east bank of the Animas. From the railroad bridge it is five more miles to the

Needle Creek Trail or six miles to Needleton. From Purgatory Campground it is a total of approximately 9.5 miles to the junction with the Needle Creek Trail or 10.5 miles to Needleton. Because most of these distances are either downhill or flat, it is possible to reach Needleton by lunch time with a reasonably early start. After lunch you can continue to reach Ruby Lake or Chicago Basin in a long day.

Needle Creek Trail

The Needle Creek Trail starts at the footbridge across the Animas at Needleton. From the bridge, one mile of flat walking south brings you to the junction with the Purgatory Creek Trail at Needle Creek, where the trail begins to gain elevation as it climbs southeast up the Needle Creek drainage. From the junction of the two trails, 1.6 miles of hiking will bring you to a spot where the trail skirts the creek. This is a favorite lunch spot for backpackers who have taken the early morning train from Durango. If you look carefully, you will spot an old water wheel on the south side of the creek. If you are interested in hiking up to Webb, Pear, or Emerald lakes, cross over the creek at this point and begin your search for the Webb Lake Trail. The Needle Creek Trail stays on the north side of Needle Creek and continues to climb up the drainage for a total of six miles from Needleton to a trail junction at 11,000 feet. If you turn right at the junction and cross over Needle Creek, you will continue for two miles and 1,700 vertical feet to the top of Columbine Pass which connects with the Johnson Creek drainage. If you continue straight ahead at the junction, you will climb into Upper Chicago Basin. From the junction, it is 1.5 miles and 1,500 vertical feet to the Twin Lakes. There are a number of excellent campsites in Chicago Basin. There is also usually a large number of backpackers and climbers in the area. If the basin is too crowded, one option is to take the righthand fork which leads up to Columbine Pass and camp in the wooded area near the foot of Jupiter Mountain near the spot where the trail turns south toward the pass. Beginning with Jupiter and continuing in a counterclockwise direction, the peaks which line Chicago Basin are Jupiter Mountain, Windom Peak, Sunlight Spire, Sunlight Peak, Peak Eleven, Twin Thumbs, Glacier Point, North Eolus, and

Mount Eolus. Located within the basin, directly west of Windom Peak, is Peak Eighteen (13,472 feet).

Webb Lake Trail

The Webb Lake Trail starts 1.6 miles east of the junction between the Needle Creek and Purgatory Creek trails, where the Needle Creek Trail meets Needle Creek near an old water wheel. The water wheel is surrounded by foliage and can be difficult to spot. At this point, cross south over Needle Creek and hike back through the woods until you find the spot where the trail begins its climb up to Webb Lake. It is difficult to estimate the mileage from Needle Creek to Webb Lake. There are no Forest Service signs to help. As the crow flies, it is about one mile, but the endless switchbacks probably make the trail closer to two miles. Although a relatively short distance, the 1,800-foot vertical gain makes this as tough a trail as you will ever care to hike. The best campsites at Webb Lake are located on the north end of the lake. The lake itself is small and shallow. From the lake, as you look south, you see two major drainages. Pear Lake is located in the lefthand drainage about .7 mile and 650 vertical feet away. Pear Lake is a beautiful, clear mountain lake. From Pear Lake, it is possible to continue .5 mile over a small rise to the east and join Emerald Lake. All three lakes afford excellent fishing. Although the USGS map indicates that there is a trail from Emerald Lake down to Needle Creek, don't be tempted to try it. My one attempt at trying to find the trail resulted in a miserable bushwhack. From Pear Lake, there is a rough trail which climbs to the pass southwest of the lake. From the pass, there is an easy climb up to Overlook Point which affords an excellent view of the main body of the Needles to the northwest.

Vallecito Creek and Johnson Creek Trails

Using this trail system, it is possible to approach the Chicago Basin peaks from the east. This trail system is generally not used as frequently by climbers as the Needle Creek approach since it typically requires a two-day backpack. Vallecito Reservoir is located thirteen miles north of Bayfield on U.S. 160 or twenty miles east of Durango on Florida Road. Once at the reservoir, stay west or left of the dam for five miles where you will come to a well-marked road junction which gives you a choice between Vallecito Campground and Pine River Campground. Turn left at the junction and drive three miles to the Vallecito Campground and trailhead. Nine miles up this part of the trail you will reach the turnoff to the Johnson Creek Trail which is located where a well-constructed bridge crosses Vallecito Creek. There are many excellent campsites in this area. From the trail junction nine miles up the Vallecito Creek Trail, the Johnson Creek Trail climbs six miles and 3,500 vertical feet to the top of Columbine Pass at 12,700 feet.

Vallecito Creek and Sunlight Creek Trails

The Sunlight Creek drainage joins Vallecito Creek twelve miles north of the trailhead. There is not a bridge across Vallecito Creek at this point and it is necessary to wade the creek before you reach Sunlight Creek. Crossing Vallecito Creek is not as serious a proposition as crossing the Animas, but it is best to plan such a trip for later in the year when the stream is lower. The trail up Sunlight Creek follows the south side of the drainage; it is important to cross over Vallecito Creek south of the point where Sunlight Creek runs into the Vallecito. There is an excellent camping area on Sunlight Creek in the last stand of timber between 11,400 feet and 11,600 feet. It is possible to cross from the Sunlight Creek drainage into the Noname Creek drainage by using the pass between Knife Point and Peak Ten or the pass just north of Jagged Mountain. A campsite high in Sunlight Creek Basin would be an excellent point of beginning for climbs of Knife Point, Peak Ten, Jagged Mountain, Leviathan Peak, and Vallecito Mountain.

Ruby Lake Trail

This is, without a doubt, one of the most difficult trails you will ever attempt to locate. It took me four attempts before I was finally able to locate and follow the trail its entire distance. From the Needleton bridge walk north about one-third of a mile (roughly six minutes at a brisk pace) along the trail on the west side of the Animas River. At this point you should reach an old metal railroad car and the floor of an old cabin. Although there is no trail in sight at this point, take a forty-five-degree turn and head northeast through the woods for about one-quarter of a mile to a point where you will reach the base of the mountains which rise from the east bank of the Animas. Traverse along the base of the slope until you spot the trail angling up the slope. The trail climbs steeply up through the woods and crosses an unnamed drainage between Pigeon Creek and Ruby Creek. At about 10,300-foot elevation, the trail crosses over the ridge which forms the south side of the Ruby Creek drainage and after losing some elevation traverses the south side of the drainage until it meets the drainage itself about three-quarters of a mile west of Ruby Lake. It then continues on the south side of the creek until you reach the lake. At Ruby Lake, the best campsites are generally on the west or north sides of the lake.

If, like many before you, you are unable to find the trail, your next best option is to hike back to the river trail, go about three-quarters to one mile up the river from the Needleton bridge, and directly ascend the ridge which forms the south side of the Ruby Creek drainage to the point at 10,300 feet elevation, where you will meet the trail as it crosses over the ridge. Whatever you do, do not attempt to climb directly up the Ruby Creek drainage. The elevation gained from the Needleton bridge to Ruby Lake is roughly 2,600 feet.

To continue into the upper portion of Ruby Creek, stay on the north side of the creek to climb the steep bench just west of the lake. After topping out on the bench, it is necessary to fight your way through a thick growth of chest-high willows until you reach easier walking higher in the drainage. A 12,700-foot pass just south of Monitor Peak connects the Ruby Creek drainage with the Noname Creek drainage. The basin above Ruby Lake provides access to Pigeon Peak, Turret Peak, Peak Fifteen, Peak Sixteen, Little Finger, Monitor Peak, Peak Thirteen, Animas Mountain, North Eolus, and The Index.

Noname Creek Trail

The mouth of Noname Creek is located two miles north of the Needleton bridge. To avoid wading the Animas, it is best to cross over to the east bank of the Animas and follow a trail on that side. There is some difficult going as the trail passes through the cliffs on Watertank Hill just south of Ruby Creek. As you might suspect, Watertank Hill is located just opposite the Needleton watertank. Once past the cliffs, however, you have smooth sailing to Noname Creek, where a well-defined trail starts out to the north of the creek. It is also possible to walk the railroad tracks from Needleton and then wade the Animas or, if you get lucky, cross logs lashed together by Outward Bound groups. The crossing can only be made late in the year and even then can be difficult. From the Animas, four miles and 2,300 vertical feet will bring you to a trail junction. Left takes you toward Peak Six and Jagged Mountain. Right leads you to Twin Thumbs Pass and the Chicago Basin peaks. The lefthand trail for Peak Six and Jagged heads east about seventy-five feet before you reach Noname Creek and climbs one-half mile to a beautiful meadow with a great view of Knife Point. In the meadow, it is necessary to make another left and head north up a steep bench, if you are interested in Peak Six and Jagged. There are several excellent campsites in the upper basin of the Noname drainage.

CLIMBING ROUTES

Mount Eolus (14,083 feet)

NORTHEAST RIDGE — From Chicago Basin contour to the left (west) into the large basin below Eolus' east face. Once high in the basin, traverse right (north) toward the plateau at 13,720 feet. From the plateau, traverse left (southwest) toward the narrow ridge connecting Eolus and North Eolus. Once on the ridge, you can choose between a direct climb of the northeast ridge or the upper part of the east face. The ridge, which is comprised of highly fractured blocks, is difficult and exposed. Care should be taken to test holds for firmness. From Twin Lakes, the 13,720-foot plateau can also be reached by a third class scramble up the steep couloir west of the lakes.

UPPER EAST FACE — This is the standard route on Eolus. From the ridge connecting Eolus and North Eolus, the route weaves its way up the upper east face. Although well-traveled and usually marked with cairns, the route can be difficult to follow. Watch for loose rock. What appear to be stable boulders can come loose with a slight touch.

WEST FACE — The west face is climbed from New York Basin. On the lower west face there are two prominent chimneys. The first ascent party started up the south (right) chimney and thus made a "tricky traverse" to the north (left) chimney. They gained the northeast ridge just north of the summit. If you are interested in the west face, it would be worth your while to look at a copy of the September 1951 issue of *Trail and Timberline* which contains a photo illustration of the route.

North Eolus (14,039 feet)

SOUTH RIDGE — From the ridge between Eolus and North Eolus, the summit is a short scramble to the north.

NORTH FACE — The January-February 1979 issue of *Climbing* contains a brief report rating the north face of North Eolus 5.7. The first ascent party found "the crux pitch so rotten that they later found a 5.8 variation around it."

Windom Peak (14,082 feet)

WEST RIDGE — The west ridge is a moderate climb which can be approached from either lower Chicago Basin or Twin Lakes. From Chicago Basin, traverse northeast (right) into the basin between Windom and Jupiter. From the basin, the easiest way to gain the ridge is to aim for the low point (13,260 feet). It is also possible to gain the ridge at the 13,400-foot saddle by a more difficult scramble. From Twin Lakes, head east in the drainage between Sunlight and Windom and then traverse southeast to gain the ridge.

Sunlight Peak (14,059 feet)

SOUTH FACE — Sunlight and Windom are frequently climbed together. When this is done, it is preferable to climb Windom

Sunlight Peak from the summit of Peak Ten. *Photo by Tim Duffy.*

George Bell on the
summit of Sunlight Spire
after its first ascent. July
1961. *Photo courtesy
George Bell.*

first and then downclimb a steep gully on the north side of
Windom's west ridge. At the bottom of the gully, traverse across
the drainage at about 13,600 feet to the south face. When
climbed alone from Twin Lakes, simply climb up the drainage on
the north (left) side of the stream. Once on the upper part of the
south face, there are several variations which will lead to the
summit. Each requires some scrambling. The true summit of
Sunlight is a large block which requires a short exposed move. If
you feel compelled to make the final move to the summit, a short
piece of rope for a belay would be welcome.

Sunlight Spire (13,995 feet)

The summit pinnacle of the spire is a sixty-foot "obelisk." The
only reported ascents of the spire have employed direct aid in
the form of expansion bolts and pitons to climb a two- to three-
inch jam crack on the northwest side of the spire. There has been

speculation that the spire "could go as a free lead," but to date, no one has reported such a feat.

Jupiter Mountain (13,830 feet)

SOUTHWEST FACE — The best way to approach Jupiter is to take the trail from Chicago Basin toward Columbine Pass. At timberline (11,640 feet), leave the trail where it turns right (south) and head directly up the grassy slopes of the southwest face. It is best to stay left (north) on the face and eventually gain the west ridge. If you plan on climbing Windom also, it is possible to save time by downclimbing the steep couloir on the north side of the west ridge.

Glacier Point (13,704 feet)

EAST FACE - SOUTHEAST RIDGE — From Twin Lakes, climb up the east face to gain the southeast ridge which you then follow to the summit.

Twin Thumbs (13,420 feet approx.)

NONAME APPROACH — In his "Revised Climber's Guide from Noname Creek," which appeared in the October 1960 issue of *Trail and Timberline*, William E. Davis describes a route for Twin Thumbs which approaches from the cirque east of the lake (11,754). Davis suggests contouring upward and to the south (right) through the lower cliffs until snow is reached. A direct ascent up the snow north of the Thumbs will lead to chimneys and slabs northeast of the summit. Davis advises that "pitons are required for protection on this route and it should not be undertaken by a party unskilled in rope handling."

Peak Eleven (13,540 feet approx.)

TWIN THUMB PASS APPROACH — Davis reports that Peak Eleven should be available from Twin Thumbs Pass "without much technical work."

Peak 13,472, "Peak Eighteen"
(½ mile west of Windom)

NORTHEAST RIDGE — From the saddle connecting Peak Eighteen with Windom, the summit is an easy scramble up this ridge.

SOUTHWEST FACE — Several routes varying in difficulty from

Alan Hamilton rappeling the south face of Peak 18 during the 1979 Chicago Mountaineers outing in Chicago Basin. *Photo by Pat Armstrong.*

5.5 to 5.7 and in length from one to four pitches have been established on the east (right) side of the face. Accounts of these climbs and a photo illustration of the routes can be found in the Spring 1980 issue of *The Chicago Mountaineer.*

Pigeon Peak (13,972 feet)

NORTHWEST BASIN — Although this route involves a difficult approach, it is the most direct and the technically easiest route on Pigeon. From Needleton, you find the elusive Ruby Lake trail and follow it up to the 10,300-foot crossing of the ridge on the south side of the Ruby Creek drainage. Rather than following the trail down to Ruby Lake, climb up the ridge to about 10,900 where you can contour southeast into the basin northwest of Pigeon. Once in the basin, follow it directly to the ridge northwest of Pigeon's summit and then skirt the final ridge to the right (west) to gain the summit.

NORTH FACE — This has long been regarded to be the "easy" way up Pigeon. To gain the route, contour west below the north face to climb the "grassy ledges" described by Ormes which lead to the northwest ridge. The north face route is by no means the walkup that some have characterized it to be. The right route is hard to find and in bad weather can be difficult. It is also possible to take a more direct route on the north face by several technical variations on the east side of the face, which are about 5.5 in difficulty and hard to protect. About the only way to protect the eastern routes are with knife blade and angle pitons. The rock is too crumbly to trust chocks.

NORTHEAST COULOIR — As described in the October 1960 issue of *Trail and Timberline*, the route ascends the first two small couloirs lying north of the east face and gains the northwest ridge about 200 feet below the summit. The first ascent party used seven pitons and reported that "the rock was fairly sound, and rockfall was a very slight hazard even with our large party."

SOUTHEAST CHIMNEY — The southeast chimney is more commonly used as a descent route for parties who wish to climb both Pigeon and Turret in a day from Ruby Creek. It is located to the left (east) about 400 feet down the couloir on the south face

Robert F. Rosebrough rappeling the southeast chimney of Pigeon Peak. *Photo by Ernie Stromeyer.*

between the twin summits. A double rope rappel is required. The first rappel anchor is a small chockstone which will have many old slings around it. From the chockstone, rappel seventy feet to a small ledge on the wall about eight feet left (west) of the chimney. The ledge can only hold two people comfortably. The second rappel is about 120 feet long. You should have knifeblade pitons or bolts on hand to protect against the possibility that the second rappel anchor no longer exists. You can't see it from the top of the first rappel. A climb of the chimney would involve delicate, hard to protect, face climbing.

Turret Peak (13,835 feet)

NORTHWEST FACE — By the northwest face, Turret is one of the easiest climbs in the Needles. From the Ruby Creek basin, climb up toward the saddle between Turret and Pigeon before angling to the left (east) toward Turret. Given the moderate nature of the northwest face, there are several variations you can take, but an ascent of the right (south) side of the face on boulders and talus, and a descent of the left (north) side of the face on scree works well.

Peak Fifteen (13,700 feet approx.)

NEW YORK BASIN APPROACH — The initial object on this route is to reach the saddle between Peaks Fifteen and Sixteen. In the September 1951 issue of *Trail and Timberline*, Henry McClintock reported "an interesting but not very difficult rock climb. We used the rope for protection on the traverses of some ledges that were exposed but most of the time did not find belaying to be necessary." The McClintock report probably somewhat underestimates the difficulty of Peak Fifteen, which is now reputed to be one of Colorado's most difficult peaks by its easiest route. You should be equipped for some lower fifth class climbing.

Peak Sixteen (13,500 feet approx.)

NEW YORK BASIN APPROACH — Peak Sixteen is the middle of the three Turret Needles east of Turret Peak. The approach begins in New York Basin and aims for the col between Peaks Fifteen and Sixteen. After the first ascent, Henry McClintock reported that from the col "Peak Sixteen was easily reached by an ordinary rock scramble."

Little Finger "Peak Seventeen"
(13,220 feet approx.)

SOUTH FACE — The south face is split by two chimneys. The first ascent party made a technical climb which started up the western (left) chimney and then traversed to the eastern (right) chimney. A detailed account of the climb together with a photo illustration of the route is contained in the September 1951 issue of *Trail and Timberline*.

Monitor Peak (13,695 feet)

EAST FACE — The intimidating 1,200-foot east face of Monitor has yielded several difficult technical routes. Although the four routes established to date cover different portions of the lower two-thirds of the face, they all converge high on the face below the "140 foot lead."

(a.) *1947 Route* — The 1947 route starts in a "very steep gully marking the lefthand margin" of the central face and works up to a junction with a very long chimney on the left, at least 450 feet above the face. From the junction the route follows the chimney to the "ominous overhang" at about two-thirds the height of the gully with two traverses being made to the right. A delicate traverse below the overhang leads to a lie-back crack which puts you on the central face where a succession of cracks and ledges lead alternately upward and to the right into the central face. About three hundred feet below the top you reach the "140 foot lead" which is difficult, hard to protect face climbing which most climbers rate at least 5.8. Above the "140 foot lead" the route follows a V-shaped chimney for about fifteen feet before gaining the edge of the rib which forms the left side of the chimney by a difficult move and then follows the very steep wall to the left of the chimney. The first ascent party placed a total of nineteen pitons. The pitons were used for protection only and not aid. The ascent was free except for a couple of shoulderstands. They noted that although the rock on the upper face was generally

The east face of Monitor Peak. From left to right, the 1947, 1976, 1968, and 1980 routes are shown. The black "plus" marks the site of the 1947 bivouac. *Photo courtesy of Joe Stettner.*

good, they encountered much loose rock in the lower face. A detailed account of this route can be found in the December 1947 *Trail and Timberline*.

(b.) 1968 Route — The 1968 route starts just to the right of the center of the face and works slightly to the right to meet the 1947 route high on the face below the "140 foot lead." A section at about mid-height required direct aid. Approximately fifteen pitons and two nuts were placed by the 1968 party which also encountered much loose rock on the lower half of the face. A short account of this climb was published in the July 1969 *Trail and Timberline*.

(c) 1976 Route — The 1976 route starts up a chimney on the central face between the 1947 and 1968 routes. Tom Norton describes the first pitch as being 5.5 climbing on loose, rotten rock with poor protection. From a chimney belay, the second pitch goes fifteen feet up a corner, across the face (5.5) into a left-sloping 5.7 jam crack, and then left to a ledge below a seventy-five-foot corner. The third pitch climbs the seventy-five-foot, left-facing corner by a 5.8 offwidth crack. The whole thing turns into a chimney at the top. It is best to exit as high as possible to the left onto a ledge and continue up two more ledges. Near the top of the pitch move left up a crack on two points of aid and then traverse right to a fixed pin and free climb up a difficult (5.9 plus) section to a belay ledge. The fourth pitch lets up in difficulty (5.5 to 5.6) and ends with some scrambling to the belay. The fifth pitch follows a seventy-five-foot chimney which is also 5.5 to 5.6. The sixth pitch is the "140 foot lead" which Norton describes as being "tricky face climbing" (5.8). The seventh pitch, which follows the chimney initially before moving out onto the steep face, is rated 5.7. The eighth and last pitch is easy but loose and should be climbed carefully.

(d.) 1980 Route — The 1980 route starts in the deep chimney at the junction between the center and right sides of the wall to the right of the 1968 route. The route climbs the chimney for a long pitch past a chockstone and then exits onto the face following a faint, left-tending groove and crack system before traversing left to the large ledge system which connects with the 1947 route just below its junction with the 1968 route. Larry Coats rates the maximum difficulty of the route at about 5.9 and considers it to be a very serious route because of the scarcity of good protection. Coats feels that the psychological crux, if not the physical, is the first fifty feet of Stettner's "140 foot lead." He

describes it as climbing a very inobvious face above an old pin which sticks three-quarters of the way out.

SOUTH BASIN - NORTH RIDGE— From Ruby Basin, the initial object is to climb up into the south basin below Monitor, Peak Thirteen, and Animas. As you reach the basin, you will see two ramps slanting left to right (west to east) below the face of Peak Thirteen. The first (lower) ramp is a third class scramble on generally solid rock. The high ramp probably also goes, but I never got a good look at it. From the top of the ramp, climb over to a point about fifty feet below the Thirteen-Monitor saddle and begin climbing on the right (west) side of the north ridge until higher when you can climb the ridge directly. From the Thirteen-Monitor saddle, the climb is third class over loose rock.

SOUTHEAST RIDGE — From the Ruby-Noname pass, the October 1960 *Trail and Timberline* suggests contouring "westward (Ruby Basin side) under the sheer cliffs of the ridge. Climb up into the first gully—it looks like a deadend. Right under the cliffs at the head of a gully a break in the steep face will be seen leading upward to the left (west). Climb up this chute onto the south-facing slopes. Contour high along these slopes just off the ridge. Don't go so high that you get stymied, but pass from gulch to gulch until forced to climb upward to the ridge. This will place you just southeast of the summit on the ridge."

Peak Thirteen "Sceptor" (13,705 feet)

SOUTH BASIN - UPPER EAST FACE— The initial approach for Peak Thirteen from Ruby Basin is the same as that for Monitor Peak. Once in the basin, take the left to right slanting ramp toward the base of the south cliffs of Peak Thirteen and then contour below them to the upper east face. Before reaching the east face, you lose about fifty feet of elevation in one spot. The east face is a third class scramble over ledges with crumbling rock.

NONAME CREEK APPROACH - UPPER EAST FACE — From Noname Creek, William E. Davis suggests in the October 1960 *Trail and Timberline* that you climb the avalanche chute "until the snow becomes so steep that everyone is uncomfortable.

Then work your way onto the exposed ledges and slabs on the northeast side (left of the couloir when looking upward). The route goes along the obvious slash on the face." From the slash you can climb the upper east face which is described above.

SOUTH BASIN - NORTHWEST RIDGE — An alternate method of climbing Peak Thirteen is to climb toward the saddle between Peak Thirteen and Point 13,620. Climb up the northwest face toward a notch of sorts, about 100 vertical feet below the summit which allows you to cross over onto the north face. You can then scramble up the north face to the summit.

Animas Mountain (13,786 feet)

SOUTH BASIN - UPPER SOUTHEAST FACE — From the south basin, the easiest way to scramble through the rock band at 13,000 feet is to the right of the prominent chimney. Once you reach the saddle between Animas and Point 13,620, start up the upper southeast face which is class two until the last 100 feet which is class three in the broad gully just east of the summit.

NORTH COULOIR — In the October 1960 issue of *Trail and Timberline*, William E. Davis described a climb "just west of the magnificent gendarme visible from Noname Creek. Before becoming hopelessly cliffed in at the head of the couloir, leave the snow and swing right (west) onto the ledges. These go directly upward to the summit. Rope, ice ax, and pitons are necessary."

The Index (13,420 feet approx.)

The Index is the prominent point located just south of the west ridge of Animas Mountain. The highest summit is the southernmost on the ridge. The climb requires fifth class climbing (probably around 5.7 or 5.8) on vertical off width cracks. The route used by the first ascent party starts on the northwest corner of the ridge and climbs over the middle summit. From the middle summit, it is necessary to rappel to the col between the middle and main summit before attaining the final pinnacle. The March 1938 *Trail and Timberline* contains a detailed route description as well as a photo illustration of the route.

Peak Twelve (13,140 feet approx.)
(1/3 mile SE of Monitor Peak)

WEST RIDGE — From the pass between Ruby and Noname creeks, the west ridge is a walkup. The last false summit is best passed by a slight downclimb to the right (south).

Knife Point (13,265 feet)

EAST FACE — To climb the east face from Noname Creek, climb up the steep slopes to the 12,860-foot pass between Knife Point and Peak Ten. From the pass the summit via the east face is a pleasant walk up sandy scree.

NORTHWEST SPUR — The northwest spur forms the left skyline of Knife Point when viewed from the Noname side. A technical route requiring some aid has been established on the spur. An account of the climb can be found in the May 1978 issue of *Trail and Timberline*.

Peak Ten (13,420 feet approx.)

SOUTHEAST FACE — Although it looks difficult, Tim Duffy reports this climb of the southeast face from a camp in the basin above Sunlight Creek "turned out to be easy and fun." Although there was some third class along the way, it was no problem without a rope. Sandy gullies offer nice walking and scrambling between the big rocks going up. As you near the summit, go around to your left (west) and behind the summit to get to nice "steps" (blocks) which give access to the summit.

SUMMIT

The route on Jagged Mountain as viewed from the pass between the Sunlight and Noname drainages, just north of Jagged. *Photo by Robert F. Rosebrough.*

Jagged Mountain (13,824 feet)

NORTH FACE — The route on Jagged truly will test your route finding ability. The initial objective when climbing Jagged is to reach the 13,020-foot pass just north of the peak, which separates the Noname and Sunlight drainages. From the pass, pick out the prominent snow couloir and make a mental note that the true summit is just right (west) of the couloir. There is a notch just to the right (west) of the true summit which you must gain but, from the pass, it is partially obscured. When viewed from the pass, the route you will follow looks very improbable.

From the pass, traverse over to the north face and begin climbing just to the right (west) of the snow couloir. Once on the north face, you will be tempted to take a sandy ramp to the right (west) which leads to a gully. Unless you are interested in the western summits, avoid the ramp at all costs. Instead, start scrambling up the face just to the right of the couloir until you are about sixty vertical feet below the couloir's top. At this point, you begin an upward traverse below the cliffs of the summit block toward the notch just west of the main summit.

From the notch you contour out onto the south face after climbing slightly. There are at least two routes that go on the upper south face. One strenuous route with good handholds goes straight up after contouring for about fifty feet. Another which is easier but more exposed traverses all the way across the south face to a twenty-foot chimney which leads to easy scrambling. The summit is flat and roomy. Jagged is lower fifth class in spots. Take a rope and a few pieces of protection.

Gray Needle (13,430 feet)

Jon Lawyer approached Gray Needle from the Noname Creek drainage and after heading toward the ridge between Gray Needle and Peak Ten climbed up the southwest flank of Gray Needle. An eighty-foot pitch of 5.5 climbing was encountered just below the shallow col between the twin summits of Gray Needle of which the left (west) summit is the highest. The summit is comprised of a large, overhanging slab on a pedestal which from the col between the two summits is best climbed in a clockwise manner. Lawyer did not see any sign of the thirty feet of expansion bolts which the 1953 first ascent party reported placing.

Leviathan Peak (13,528 feet)

SOUTHWEST RIDGE — The southwest ridge is a rocky climb involving some third class scrambling in spots. The one thing you need to remember is to bypass the 13,420-foot false summit to the left (west).

SOUTH COULOIR — The south couloir tops out between the 13,420-foot false summit and the true summit. The couloir is filled with talus and care shold be taken to avoid dislodging it.

The Needle Mountains in winter as viewed from Snowdon Peak. *Photo by Robert F. Rosebrough.*

Vallecito Mountain (13,428 feet)

WEST RIDGE — On the lower portion of the west ridge, it is best to scramble left (north) of the ridge before gaining the top of the ridge. Follow the ridge directly to the top thereafter, except to skirt a couple of small ridge humps to the left (north). A few spots of moderate scrambling break up what is otherwise a walkup.

Peak Six (13,705 feet)

SOUTHWEST RIDGE — From the 12,900-foot pass between Peaks Five and Six, the southwest ridge is a walkup over large talus.

Peak Five (13,283 feet)

NORTHEAST RIDGE — The northeast ridge begins at the 12,900-foot pass between Peaks Five and Six. The Chicago Mountaineers reported that when climbed by this ridge, "the upper section of the peak offered pleasant scrambling with a nice friction slab near the summit."

Peak Four (13,410 feet)

SOUTH FACE — From the meadows at 10,800 in Noname Creek, William E. Davis suggests in the October 1960 issue of *Trail and Timberline* that Peak Four should be climbed by the prominent gully running north of the meadows. To gain the summit ridge it is best to keep just to the east (right) of the gully. Once on top, it is a short traverse to Peak Four.

The Heisspetz (13,262 feet)

SOUTHEAST RIDGE — Davis suggests climbing Heisspetz by the same gully as for Peak Four and then "go along the ridge to the lower summit to the west."

Wham Ridge on Vestal Peak as seen from Arrow Peak. Whitney Borland in foreground. The photo was taken four days before the first ascent of Wham Ridge during the 1941 CMC outing. *Photo by Werner Schnackenberg.*

GRENADIER RANGE

The Grenadiers exemplify the best that the San Juans have to offer. They are remote, rugged, and beautiful. Steep faces and hard quartzite make for the highest concentration of quality rock climbs in the San Juans.

The main spine of the Grenadiers runs west to east from Electric Peak, Arrow, Vestal, the Trinities, Storm King Peak, and Mount Silex to the Guardian. Arrow and Vestal are the most celebrated of the Grenadiers. Arrow had for some time been reputed to be the most difficult major mountain in Colorado to climb. This reputation was created by the rugged south face which early climbers felt was the easiest route on the peak. A less demanding route on the northeast rib has since been established, thereby casting doubt on this claim. Vestal's reputation is largely based upon its beauty. Vestal's north face, Wham Ridge, has to be seen to be believed.

Electric Peak, Graystone Peak, Point Pun, and Mount Garfield are some of the least frequently climbed peaks in Colorado. Located on the west end of the Grenadiers, they are the most inaccessible peaks in a remote range.

The east end of the main spine is formed by three high thirteen thousand-foot peaks which sport steep fifteen hundred-foot north faces: Storm King Peak, Mount Silex, and The Guardian.

To the south of Storm King Peak, Peaks Seven, Eight, and Nine connect the Grenadiers to the Needle Mountains. To the north, Peaks One, Two, Three, and White Dome separate the Grenadiers from the Continental Divide.

CLIMBING HISTORY

The inaccessibility and ruggedness of the Grenadiers combined for many years to prevent incursions. The Grenadiers were one of the few areas in the San Juans which were not climbed by either the Wheeler or Hayden survey teams. Although the surveyors did not climb in the Grenadiers, the range occupied their thoughts. The surveyors generally referred to the Grenadiers and neighboring Needles as the "Quartzites." The comments of the early surveyors were filled with feelings of fear, foreboding, and respect. Marshall's report for the Wheeler Survey noted:

> No where in Colorado can be found such steep slopes, such shapeless crags, such rocky and impassable ravines, such generally detestable characteristics and features as are here seen. The hard metamorphic rocks are shivered along their cleavage planes for hundreds of feet, leaving their odd pinnacles, there the likeness of the shattered outspread wings of some gigantic bird, and again of the grim grinning teeth of death.[1]

Marshall admitted that his "condemnation" of the quartzites stemmed from the fact that he was "deeply prejudiced against them" because of a "disagreeable experience." In early October 1874, Marshall's party was attempting to establish a triangulation station on the fringes of the range when they were trapped above timberline for three days by an early season snowstorm which left between "eighteen inches to 4 and 5 feet" of snow.

Although the Hayden team did not go so far as to "condemn" the range, they certainly shared somewhat similar feelings.

Speaking of the view from the summit of Mount Sneffels, Rhoda of the Hayden Survey reported:

> The group of quartzite peaks stood out as boldly as ever about thirty miles to the southeast. In fact, I may state here that we have never yet seen a group from any station (and we have viewed it from all sides) without feeling both deep respect and awe for their terrible ruggedness. The fact already stated, that the storm clouds seem to hover about them before starting on their meandering ways, only served to add to our other feelings of uneasiness.[2]

The closest that either of the survey teams came to climbing on the main peaks of the Grenadiers was the Hayden Survey's climb of White Dome just north of the Grenadiers. Wilson and Rhoda rode to within 1,000 feet of the summit and then climbed "over the steep debris slides before reaching the top."[3] From the summit of White Dome the Grenadiers formed a "row of ten distinct peaks stretching in a nearly east and west line before our eyes."[4]

The first climbers to reach the Grenadiers were William S. Cooper and John Hubbard in 1908. From the summit of Pigeon Peak in the Needles, Cooper's attention had been drawn to "that wonderful line of quartzite peaks dominated by Arrow and Vestal, the summits of which from our distance appeared inaccessible."[5] Cooper and Hubbard camped at Balsam Lake and climbed to the saddle between Vestal and Arrow peaks. They climbed Vestal by a rock gully on the south face which "proved interesting, but fairly easy."[6]

The south face of Arrow was an entirely different matter. Cooper noted that "Arrow Peak proved to be really difficult. Several times our holds depended on the strength of our fingers. I rather think, too, that we found the easiest route."[7]

Cooper and Hubbard did not write an account of their climbs at that time and hence, when Carleton Long and John E. Nelson climbed Arrow Peak twenty-four years later in 1932, they thought that they were the first party to do so. Long and Nelson also approached Arrow from the south. "Difficult, and at times precarious climbing," eventually led them to what Long described as a "perfectly delicious overhang."[8] Long noted that "most overhangs are things to be shunned but this particular 'hang has to its credit certain admirably placed foot and hand holds which makes its climbing easy and pleasant. The position is

Carleton Long on the summit of Arrow Peak, 1932. *Photo by John E. Nelson.*

John E. Nelson and the rugged south face of Arrow Peak just before the peak's second ascent in 1932. *Photo courtesy of John E. Nelson.*

sensational in the extreme, and any one subject to acrophobia should not attempt it."[9]

It is only appropriate that this obstacle has since been given the name "Long's Overhang." During their trip, Long and Nelson made first ascents of Point Pun and the Heisspitz. They are also credited with naming Vestal's north face Wham Ridge. After studying Wham Ridge intently for several minutes from the top of Arrow, Nelson muttered, "I still don't believe it!"[10]

After years of neglect, the Grenadiers became a very popular spot in 1941. That summer the Colorado Mountain Club held its twenty-eighth annual summer outing in the Grenadiers. Camp was located one-quarter mile below Balsam Lake in the Tenmile Creek drainage. During the outing, first ascents were made of West and Middle Trinity peaks, Storm King Peak, Peak Four, Peak Five, and Peak Seven. The biggest climb of the outing, however, was the first ascent of Wham Ridge by Rit Burrows, Werner Schnackenberg, and Jim Patterson. After a warm-up climb of Arrow by the south face, they glissaded down the snowfield on the north face of Arrow and walked over to the base of Wham Ridge.

The first several hundred feet went easily until the "gradient increased" and they were forced to rope up. In spite of fog and light rain, the party reached the summit of Vestal, after using only one piton for protection, in three hours of actual climbing time.[11]

After the 1941 outing, the Grenadiers were again neglected until interest in the area was renewed in the early 1960s. In September 1962, John C. Ohrenschall and Doug Ward were lured to the area by Burrow's report of the first ascent of Wham Ridge. Ohrenschall and Ward made several technical climbs during their stay in the Grenadiers, including the northeast face of Vestal, the east face of Arrow Peak, and the north face of West Trinity Peak. They also made what was probably the first ascent of Electric Peak by a technical route on the east face.

The next challenge which lured climbers into the Grenadiers was winter climbing. A strong team of Harvard Mountaineers consisting of David Roberts, Matt Hale, Larry Muir, Steve Pomerance, Burt Redmayne, and Don Jensen spent their 1963 Christmas vacation in the Grenadiers. After two days of snowshoeing, the party reached Vestal Lake. The group of six split up into pairs and made ascents of the southwest ridge of West Trinity, the southeast ridge of Vestal, the west ridge of Vestal, the south face of Arrow, the south ridge of Storm King,

John Ohrenschall on the east face of Electric Peak during the peak's first ascent in 1962. *Photo by Doug Ward.*

the southwest ridge of Peak Eight, and the south face of East Trinity Peak. Roberts and Jensen's climb of Peak Eight is noteworthy for the fact that it may have been a first ascent for any season. Roberts noted that there "was not the slightest pile of rocks on either summit, and after searching through the snow meticulously, we could find no trace of visitation."[12]

Roberts and Jensen had used a rope and several pitons on the climb and Roberts also noted that "We feel that our route, with one possible exception, is the easiest on the peak, and it was none too easy."[13]

Although most of the routes taken by the Harvard Mountaineers would be difficult under any conditions, Roberts felt that the south face of East Trinity involved the most technically difficult climbing.

One route which the Harvard Mountaineers did not touch was Wham Ridge. The first winter ascent of Wham Ridge was left to Arthur Mears, Don Vasicek, Steve Tandy, John Pinamont, and Tom Ruwitch in January of 1968. This strong party was slowed by the steepness of the upper ridge and did not reach the summit until sunset. "It was a strangely subdued party that stood on Vestal Peak's summit that evening."[14] After being forced to bivouac high on the south ridge they made it down without trouble the next day.

During the late 1960s and 1970s, many multiple-pitch technical routes were established on the steep faces of the Grenadiers. In August 1968, Martin Etter and Sam Casey climbed the northwest face of Arrow Peak via the Arrowhead pinnacle on Arrow's west shoulder. In August of 1969, Etter teamed with Bo Shelby to climb a direct route on the east face of Vestal Peak. In July of 1971, Henry Barber and Tom Stimson climbed the north saddle between West and Middle Trinity.

The first ascent of the 1,500-foot north face of Storm King was made in August 1974 by Bob Bliss and Don Jones. Bliss had climbed five pitches on the northeast shoulder in late August 1966 with Andy Lichtman, only to be forced into retreat by a hailstorm. Although warned by Larry Dalke that "those faces are to be looked at, not climbed," Bliss returned and was surprised to find a "path of ledges, short cracks and chimneys, leading up and right for hundreds of feet, all hidden before by a plate of rock."[15]

These long, hard routes exemplify the current trend of climbing in the Grenadiers. More than any other area in the San

Bob Bliss belaying the first pitch of Storm King's north face during its first ascent. *Photo courtesy of Bob Bliss.*

Juans, the Grenadiers offer an abundance of high-quality, multiple-pitch climbs.

Notes

1. Wheeler, Annual Report of the Chief Engineers for 1876, Appendix JJ, p. 101.
2. Rhoda, *Summits to Reach*, p. 75.
3. *Ibid.*, p. 57.
4. *Ibid.*
5. William S. Cooper, Unpublished Manuscript entitled "Mountains," p. 68.
6. *Ibid.*, p. 71.
7. *Ibid.*, p. 72.
8. *T&T*, November 1932.
9. *Ibid.*

10. *T&T*, February 1941.
11. *T&T*, October 1941.
12. *T&T*, July 1964.
13. *Ibid*.
14. *T&T*, January 1969.
15. Personal Correspondence, Bob Bliss.

ACCESS AND HIKING

Molas Trail - Lower Elk Creek Trail - Vestal Creek

This is the most popular means of access to the Grenadiers. The initial object of this route is to reach Elk Park on the Animas River. Elk Park is a regular stop for the narrow gauge train between Durango and Silverton. The train reaches Elk Park at 11:20 a.m. and returns on its way back to Durango at 2:20 p.m. To flag it down, stand on the siding (east) side of the tracks. Information on reservations and general policies of the railroad can be found under the access heading for the Needles.

For those not interested in riding the train, the best way to reach Elk Park is by the Molas Trail, which starts one and one-quarter miles north of Molas Pass between Durango and Silverton on U.S. 550 (six miles south of Silverton).

The trailhead starts from a gravel road just south of Molas Lake. From the trailhead, the trail (which at first is a dirt road) takes off south and then traverses east through several large meadows as you begin the descent to the Animas River. Although it is only about two or two and one-half miles as the crow flies, there are over thirty switchbacks in the trail which make the total walking distance more like four miles.

The trail starts at 10,600 feet elevation and drops 1,700 feet to 8,900 feet at Elk Park. After you cross the bridge across the Animas and the railroad track, a trail angles off to the left where, after three-quarters of a mile, it meets the Elk Creek Trail coming

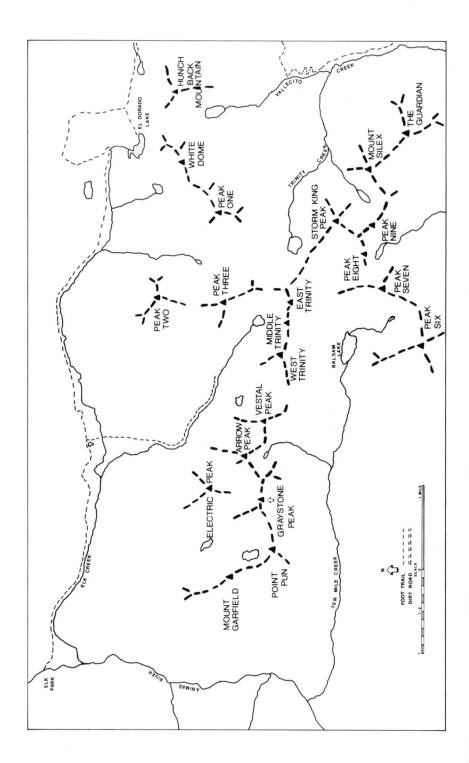

up from Elk Park. It is also possible to walk the tracks down to Elk Park and then follow the Elk Creek Trail from its start, but this is not recommended since it is necessary to climb the steep bench to the east of Elk Park over a shorter distance.

Once on the Elk Creek Trail, follow it east for three miles to a group of beaver ponds. Immediately after passing the beaver ponds, turn right and follow a faint trail which makes a U-turn around the beaver ponds and heads south to cross Elk Creek and leads to the Vestal Creek drainage. The crossing of Elk Creek is made by downclimbing into the steep gorge and walking across a couple of logs at the bottom. This unmaintained trail climbs left (east) of Vestal Creek before meeting it about a mile up the drainage. It is worthwhile to take your time in finding the trail because the climb up Vestal Creek without it is miserable.

About a mile and a half up Vestal Creek you will reach some marshy meadows below Arrow Peak at 11,400 feet. A wooded bench on the northern fringe of the meadows offers camping as do the woods on the east end of the meadows at the foot of the steep bench. A campsite in this area is probably the best point of beginning for both Arrow and Vestal peaks. It is also possible to continue up the trail for another quarter-mile up a steep bench to some wooded campsites below Vestal at 11,600 feet. The approach by Vestal Creek is the best access for Arrow Peak and Vestal Peak. It is also a good means of access for the Trinity Peaks. Graystone Peak, Electric Peak, Point Pun, and Mount Garfield can be reached from Vestal Creek by climbing up into the drainage between Arrow and Electric peaks. Peaks Two and Three can also be climbed from a campsite in Vestal Creek.

From Vestal Creek it is possible to reach the Tenmile Creek drainage and Balsam Lake by the 12,860-foot pass between Vestal and West Trinity. It is also possible to connect with Trinity Creek and Stormy Gulch by continuing east up Vestal Creek to the 12,980-foot pass at the head of the drainage. This pass looks very difficult from low in the drainage but actually is not that bad. When coming up from Vestal Creek, it is best to attack the pass from the left.

Tenmile Creek

Tenmile Creek is named not for its length but for its distance from Silverton. The Colorado Mountain Club built a trail in 1941 as part of its outing in the Grenadier area. The trail has since been unmaintained and is reported to be very difficult to find in places. To reach Tenmile Creek you begin by hiking two and a half miles south on the railroad tracks from Elk Park. The railroad tracks are located on the east side of the Animas River at Elk Park but cross over to the west side of the Animas about three-quarters of a mile south of Elk Park. Don't be tempted to leave the tracks and stay on the east side of the Animas as it is "nearly impossible" to reach Tenmile Creek from the east side of the Animas. It is necessary to wade the Animas and, hence, this approach is best used in late August or early September. Don't even consider this route during the spring or early summer. Ormes notes that the crossing "is impossible for anyone without otters in the family tree."

Once across the Animas, the trail up Tenmile Canyon starts on the south side of Tenmile Creek and continues up the creek for 1.5 miles where it crosses over to the north side. About two miles up the creek, a steep water course gives access to Point Pun. The total distance from the Animas to Balsam Lake is four miles. From the Animas, the trail starts at 8,200 feet and climbs to 11,400 feet for a total vertical gain of 3,200 feet. Balsam Lake provides access for climbs of the Trinity Peaks, Peak Seven, Peak Eight, Peak Nine, and Storm King Peak.

Vallecito Creek Trail

Vallecito Creek Trail is a popular trail which provides access for peaks on the eastern end of the Grenadier Range. Vallecito Reservoir is located thirteen miles north of Bayfield on U.S. 160 and twenty miles east of Durango on Florida Road. Once past the dam, stay west (left) of the lake for five miles where you will come to a well-marked road junction which gives you a choice between Vallecito Campground and Pine River Campground. Turn left at the junction and drive another three miles to the trailhead at Vallecito Campground.

The first mile of the trail climbs steeply and affords fine views of the spectacular Vallecito Creek Gorge. The trail starts on the west side of Vallecito Creek and crosses over to the east on a bridge at three miles and then back to the west at slightly over five miles. At 6.5 miles the trail crosses a third bridge. At nine miles a trail takes off to the left and heads up Johnson Creek to Columbine Pass and Chicago Basin. For the Grenadiers stay on the main Vallecito Trail which continues north on the east side of the river. After a total of 15.5 miles, you will reach Stormy Gulch and Trinity Creek. Trinity Creek drains the north sides of Storm King Peak, Mount Silex, The Guardian, and Peak Nine. From Vallecito Creek it is three miles up to the 12,980-foot pass at the head of Trinity Creek Basin which connects with Vestal Creek. After hiking about a mile up Stormy Gulch, it is possible to climb to Lake Silex which is located in a semi-circle formed by Storm King Peak, Peak Nine, and Mount Silex. The total distance from Vallecito Creek to Lake Silex is 1.8 miles. From Lake Silex it is another steep .3 mile to the northwest to a 12,820-foot pass between Storm King Peak and Peak Eight which connects you with the upper end of the Tenmile Creek drainage and Balsam Lake.

Although you should count on hiking for a day and a half or two days, the Vallecito Creek Trail is the best means of access for Mount Silex and The Guardian. It is also good for Storm King Peak, Peak Eight, and Peak Nine.

Vallecito Creek Trail can also be used as a means of access for White Dome and Peak One. Rather than turning west at Stormy Gulch, continue on Vallecito Creek drainage for another three-quarters of a mile and then turn left and follow the trail up the Vallecito Creek drainage which turns off the main trail. The main trail turns right near the junction between Nebo Creek and Vallecito Creek and continues north to Hunchback Pass. Instead of following the main trail, turn left and hike up the steep Vallecito Creek drainage to Vallecito Lake at 12,010 feet.

Upper Elk Creek Trail

From the beaver ponds, three miles east of Elk Park, the trail continues up the north side of Elk Creek for a total of 7.5 miles from the Animas, where it levels out at 12,100 feet near an old mining cabin above timberline. From this point the trail turns north toward the Continental Divide. For access to the peaks north of the Grenadiers, it is best to leave the trail and turn southeast at the old mining cabin, head southeast, and contour east to Eldorado Lake or continue south to the 12,780-foot pass between White Dome and Hunchback Mountain. From the pass it is then possible to drop down into Vallecito Lake. The pass also provides a convenient point from which it is possible to climb both White Dome and Hunchback Mountain.

Cunningham Gulch and Continental Divide Trails

The combination of these two trails provides an alternate means of access to White Dome and Peak One. By road, travel four miles northeast from Silverton to Howardsville. From Howardsville turn right and drive 3.6 miles up Cunningham Gulch to the remains of the Highland Mary Mill. Near the old mill, the road crosses the stream and should only be driven by four-wheel drive. After about .3 mile the road crosses Cunningham Gulch to the left. Cunningham Gulch trail takes off to the left near the crossing and climbs for two miles from 10,800 to 12,200 feet where it intersects the Continental Divide Trail. Don't be tempted to follow the road, which soon turns into a trail, or you will end up at Highland Mary Lakes. From the junction with the Continental Divide Trail, hike 4.6 miles south, above timberline to a point where you can drop west to Eldorado Lake or continue south between Hunchback Mountain and White Dome to Vallecito Lake.

Noname Creek

The trail up Noname Creek is described under the section on the Needles. From Noname Creek the 12,900-foot pass between Peak Five and Peak Six gives access to Ten Mile Creek and Balsam Lake.

CLIMBING ROUTES

Mount Garfield (13,074 feet)

SOUTHEAST RIDGE — From a camp in Vestal Creek, the best approach for Garfield is to climb into the drainage between Electric and Arrow peaks. From the 12,460-foot saddle between Electric and Graystone peaks take a high traverse around the northern face of Graystone over steeply angled, smooth slabs. When dry, the slabs make for a fast traverse. When wet or blocked by snow early in the year, the traverse can be difficult. After finishing the traverse and reaching Garfield Lake, climb steeply up to the saddle between Mount Garfield and Point Pun. Garfield's southeast ridge is a deceptively long ridge climb with class three scrambling. The scrambling is made enjoyable by the general lack of exposure. Stay directly on the ridge with only very slight deviations.

Point Pun (13,180 feet approx.)

NORTH FACE — The initial approach for Point Pun is the same as that for Mount Garfield, except that after finishing with the smooth slabs on the traverse, you should turn south and climb a little bit to gain a 12,640-foot bench on the west flank of Graystone Peak.

Point Pun is comprised of two summits of which the eastern summit is higher. Inexplicably, USGS gives an exact elevation for the lower western summit but not the higher one. The north face of the eastern summit is a hard third class scramble over lichen-covered rock. Steep foot and handholds are plentiful. Unfortunately, a few of them tend to be a little loose.

If you wish to combine Mount Garfield with Point Pun, you can traverse the western summit to the north on a talus-covered ledge system. The western summit of Point Pun is best climbed by its northwest ridge which Mike Butyn describes as being fourth class. It is difficult to combine both summits of Point Pun because of the cliffs on the eastern side of the western summit. The ridge connecting Mount Garfield to Point Pun is a cakewalk.

Graystone Peak (13,489 feet)

NORTHEAST RIDGE — This route starts at the 12,980-foot pass between Arrow and Graystone. The pass can be gained from either side, but is steeper from the west. From the pass, walk up the ridge to the northwest end of Peak 13,404 and then turn west and scramble along the ridge toward Graystone's east face. Head directly up the face toward the false summit and then traverse right onto the north face before climbing to the true summit.

NORTH COULOIR — This couloir runs directly up the north face of Graystone between the two rounded summits. The couloir makes for a steep snow climb for which ice ax and crampons are recommended. Later in the year, when the couloir becomes discontinuous at several points, it is necessary to climb right (west) to regain the snow. The couloir is usually not worth messing with after early August. From the top of the couloir, the summit is a walkup.

Electric Peak (13,292 feet)

SOUTH FACE — The route on the south face of Electric starts from the 12,460-foot saddle between Electric and Graystone and climbs up to the lefthand (west) couloir. Scramble up the couloir, traverse to the right (east), and then climb directly up the talus field to the rounded summit. Care should be taken while in the couloir not to set off any of the loose rock.

EAST FACE — A fourteen pitch route of lower fifth class climbing was reported in the June 1963 *Trail and Timberline*. The east face is a narrow face between the "tree studded northeast face" and the "sheer southeast face." Begin the climb from the lefthand (south) end of the large grass patch, uphill from the base of the northeast face. A chimney on the lower face is passed to the right. From the chimney, traverse right to a gully system which is climbed to a platform overlooking the sheer southeast face. From the platform, climb to the right to a ramp leading up and to the left. Continue up the ramp to the talus field leading to the summit.

Arrow Peak (13,803 feet)

NORTHEAST RIB — Although certainly no walkup, this is the easiest route on Arrow. The route follows either of two prominent ribs (the larger eastern rib is frequently blocked by a large snowbank early in the season) to within 400 feet of the summit. From this point, one can either climb right (west) and reach the summit by skirting the north ridge to the east or by climbing the final portion of the northeast face directly. The direct ascent of the northeast face is the more difficult variation. The view of Wham Ridge on Vestal from this route is amazing.

Arrow Peak. The northeast rib route starts just above the lower right-hand corner of the photo. *Photo by Ernie Stromeyer.*

SOUTH FACE — From the west end of Arrow Lake go north and a little west to the parallel gullies on the west side of the south face. Take the righthand (east) gully. Near the top, just below a band of red rocks, you reach Long's overhang. At this point, either climb the overhang or climb left, up and over a vertical slab, into a short chimney fifteen feet west of the overhang. Rope and protection are recommended.

NORTHWEST FACE — The October 1969 *Trail and Timberline* reports a climb of the northwest face via the Arrowhead pinnacle on Arrow's west shoulder. The route starts at the lowest point at the base of the west face and climbs eleven or twelve pitches to the top of the pinnacle. From the pinnacle a "60 foot rappel into the notch is followed by 150 feet of scrambling to the main summit." The route is rated III 5.7.

EAST FACE — The east face is cut diagonally by two "parabolic appearing curves." The route, as reported in the June 1963 *Trail and Timberline*, starts on the lower or southern ramp and traverses right to a ledge and gully system which parallels the ramp. Ascend the ledge and gully system for two or three leads and traverse right to a crack system for two pitches to a sloping grass-filled crack. Traverse left to a large platform. The last pitch climbs slightly right to the easy summit slopes. There are a total of eight pitches of lower fifth class climbing.

NORTH RIDGE — Michael Covington reports that Arrow's north ridge is a good fifth class climb. From the lower meadows camping area, the long north ridge can be seen rising from the canyon below. At an elevation equal to that of the lower meadow is a band of trees diagonally from left to right, leading onto the ridge. Although the climbing amongst the trees is easy, a slip would be disastrous. After climbing three rope pitches up through the trees, you reach the upper band of trees leading out onto the north ridge. Once on the ridge, five pitches ranging from fourth class to 5.6 on excellent rock are followed by two loose, fourth class pitches. After the two fourth class pitches, scramble hundreds of feet to the final summit ridge. For protection, a selection of eight chocks ranging in size from a #8 hex to a number 2 stopper will suffice. All belays were on good ledges or stances, but the anchors on about the sixth pitch are difficult to obtain. Covington mentioned that if he were to do the climb again, he would walk down the trail about one-half

Roped climbing on Arrow's north ridge. *Photo by Michael Covington.*

mile and begin the climb at the very toe of the buttress. He feels this probably would add another four good pitches.

Vestal Peak (13,864 feet)

SOUTHEAST COULOIR — The easiest route on Vestal ascends the large couloir on the eastern side of the south face. From the saddle between Arrow and Vestal, the couloir is out of view behind the rock rib which runs directly down the south face from the summit. From the saddle, traverse upward across the lower face to the couloir and follow the couloir to the top. This route is not particularly difficult, but it does involve scrambling over large boulders and some loose rock.

David Nordstrom and Ike Weaver getting ready to take on Vestal Peak's Wham Ridge. *Photo by Robert F. Rosebrough.*

WHAM RIDGE — Wham Ridge is not a ridge but a huge triangular buttress. Although it appears smooth as glass from a distance, the rock is actually "highly fissured." Although some parties climb Wham Ridge third class, a rope and several pieces of protection are recommended, particularly in threatening weather. The rock on the lower portion of the route is excellent. Higher up, the rock is more broken up and a little loose in spots. There are countless variations you can take, but a route which starts just to the right of the prominent dihedral in the center of the face and works slightly to the right (west) works well. Regardless of which variation you take, you should, by judicious route finding, avoid anything over 5.3 or 5.4 in difficulty.

EAST FACE — A direct route reported in the October 1969 *Trail and Timberline* starts at the base of a dihedral in orange

Ike Weaver and David Nordstrom nearing the middle section of Wham Ridge. *Photo by Robert F. Rosebrough.*

rock just left of the low point of the face. The first two leads are the most difficult. The first is sustained 5.8 up the dihedral to a small ledge on the right wall above the prominent overhang. The second lead involves aid for a short distance and then several difficult moves to the large, left-slanting ledge that dissects the entire face. From the top of the ledge (200 feet long) climb right on a steep ledge to a sharp corner. One and a half easy pitches lead to the east summit which is only a scramble away from the true summit. The direct route is rated III 5.8, A-1. The *Trail and Timberline* report indicates that there are also several variations on the east face which are much easier than this direct line.

The Trinity Peaks as viewed from the summit of Peak 7 during the 1941 CMC outing. *Photo by Werner Schnackenberg.*

West Trinity Peak (13,765 feet)

SOUTHWEST RIDGE — The southwest ridge is the standard route on West Trinity when approached from Vestal Creek. It is also the beginning for a traverse of the Trinities which is best attempted from west to east. The climbing on the ridge consists of good third class scrambling. The route generally follows the ridge or stays just to the right (south) of the ridge crest.

SOUTHEAST FACE — The upper southeast face is the most direct route on West Trinity when approached from Balsam Lake. A moderate scramble to the left (south) of the southeast ridge brings you to the summit.

NORTH FACE — In the view of the Grenadiers from Molas Lake on U.S. 550, West Trinity's north face appears very similar to Wham Ridge which, from this view, is hidden behind Electric Peak. According to Michael Covington, the pitches on the north face are all fourth class or very low fifth class. Although Covington chose a line just to the right of the center of the face and climbed up eight pitches on a gradual right to left diagonal, he reports that by the looks of it, you can wander around most anywhere on the face and come up with an easy route. A selection of five chocks including a #8 hex and several runners will suffice for belay anchors or protection, if required.

NORTH SADDLE — There have been several climbs reported on the 600-foot wall north of the saddle, between West and Middle Trinity. The January-February 1972 issue of *Climbing* reports a route named Mass Gyration on the "Trinity North Saddle." The route description advised one to "go up farthest set of crack systems on the right. Several overhangs and bulges after broken up rock at bottom. Pitches 7, NCCS II, F6 or F7."

The January-February 1971 issue of *Summit* also describes a technical climb on the north saddle "which started on an enticing crack on the west side." The route passes over a double overhang on the second pitch and then follows a diagonal ledge to the left. Near the top the route followed "two ripple-like ledges which traversed 250 feet to the top of the wall." No difficulty rating was given.

A climb rated NCCS III, F8 which "started near the center of the wall and went slightly right in wide, grassy cracks and grooves toward a slot on the ridge crest formed by opposite-facing dihedrals" was reported in the 1981 *American Alpine Journal*. This party "climbed six pitches, the last three being the steepest and most difficult, sometimes with little protection."

Middle Trinity Peak (13,805 feet)

WEST RIDGE — This route is, without a doubt, the most difficult section of a traverse of the Trinities. It involves some challenging fourth class climbing and will put your route finding abilities to the test. When traversing over from West Trinity, stay as high as possible below the cliffs on the south side of the sharp ridge between the peaks. As you pass the saddle between the two peaks, begin an upward traverse staying as high as possible below the cliffs of the west ridge. Keep a sharp eye out for cairns which will lead you to a broken up chimney which tops out on some ledges and allows you to either scramble over or traverse to the south of the 13,700-foot false summit which is called "The Fourth Trinity" by some. Once past the false summit, the last section to the true summit is easy.

Traversing the ridge between West Trinity and Middle Trinity during the 1941 CMC outing. *Photo by Werner Schnackenberg.*

EAST COULOIR — The east couloir is a relatively easy scramble but caution should be taken with loose rock. Once a rock is set loose, it tends to fall the full length of the couloir. For that reason, hard hats and small parties, closely grouped, are preferable. When descending, as part of a traverse, stay left (north) when the couloir branches halfway down.

East Trinity Peak (13,745 feet)

WEST COULOIR — The west couloir is a broad gully which covers the entire west face of the East Trinity. As seems to be the case with almost every Trinity route, the west couloir involves third class scrambling over some loose rock. The easiest variation is to stay to the right (south) to gain the final ridge which takes you to the top. Early in the year, snow probably will force you to the middle of the couloir.

NORTHEAST RIDGE — This is a good descent route for a west to east traverse. When East Trinity is climbed alone, this is the best route from Vestal Creek. The climb starts at the 13,060-foot notch on the ridge between Vestal Creek and Trinity Creek. Easy to moderate scrambling leads you to the summit.

SOUTH FACE — A difficult fifth class route which offers "perfect clean ledges for holds" was reported in the July 1964 *Trail and Timberline*. The first ascent party was "in love with rock" which was "as firm as Peak 8's had been rotten." The route meets the southeast ridge 400 feet below the summit.

Storm King Peak (13,752 feet)

SOUTHWEST RIDGE — From the 12,820-foot pass which connects Tenmile Creek to the Lake Silex drainage, scramble directly up the ridge over large boulders and loose rock.

NORTH FACE — Storm King's north face is a dark, intimidating 1,500-foot wall. Given its appearance, Bob Bliss was surprised to find what he describes as a "gentle flower-strewn-path-of-a-climb." Bliss's route starts below the central block streak and climbs forty feet to a ramp. From the ramp, climb right (west) up third and fourth class ledges and short chimneys and then seventy feet up broken wet rock to a formation which Bliss describes as a "bowl of tears." At this point you climb up a steep left-facing slab or dihedral and then four pitches up a chimney-crack behind a great plate. Traverse sixty feet right (west) below the "plate glass" smooth slabs and then up ninety feet via a crack in a left-facing dihedral with a small wet overhang at the top (5.7).

Three long leads of third and fourth class climbing lead to snow and then up left (east) to a "pass" climbing on mud. From the "pass," a pitch of poorly protected shattered quartzite and two more easy pitches up broken blocks lead to the summit ridge. There are a total of fifteen pitches rated IV, 5.7.

Mount Silex (13,628 feet)

SOUTH FACE — The starting point for this climb is the 12,820-foot pass between Mount Silex and point 13,176. When approached from Tenmile Creek, it is possible to make a rugged traverse toward the saddle several hundred vertical feet above Lake Silex to the south. Rather than fighting the traverse, however, I prefer to drop down almost to the lake. On the climb to the pass most of the scree and talus can be avoided by kicking steps up the snowbank and scrambling on the rock above. No matter how you try, some of the scree and talus is unavoidable. To gain the south face, which is the easiest route on Mount Silex, from the pass it is necessary to lose about 400 vertical feet before you can traverse through the cliff band on the lower portion of the face. After clearing the cliffs, the south face is a class two talus climb. If you are interested in climbing The Guardian in the same day, you are best to downclimb this route before starting the rugged traverse east.

SOUTHWEST RIDGE — From the 12,820-foot pass, the southwest ridge leads directly to the summit. The lower portion of the ridge consists of rugged fourth or lower fifth class climbing over steep rock with good holds. There is also a rough section at mid-height which can be easily avoided by making a detour onto the south face.

SOUTHEAST RIDGE — The lower two-thirds of the southeast ridge are cliffs which force you into some fourth class climbing just to the south. For the last couple of hundred yards you can gain and keep the ridge to the summit.

EAST FACE — The January-February 1979 issue of *Climbing* reports a "fine 18 pitch route" rated 5.7. No other details about the route are given.

The Guardian (13,617 feet)

SOUTHWEST COULOIR - NORTHWEST RIDGE — From just below the saddle between The Guardian and Peak 13,220, make an upward traverse below the cliffs of the northwest ridge. At about 13,350 you will spot a talus-filled couloir running straight up to the northwest ridge. Follow the couloir to the ridge. At the top of the couloir, you scramble through some broken up rock to reach the easier ridge above and walk to the summit. As you might suspect, given its location, the summit affords an excellent view of the Vallecito Creek drainage.

Peak Two (13,475 feet)

SOUTHWEST RIDGE — From 11,400 feet in the Vestal Creek drainage across from Vestal Peak, climb up the steep north side of the drainage which flattens out at 12,800. Once on top, walk over to the 12,940-foot saddle between Peaks Three and Four. The saddle also can be reached by climbing up the scree from the Elk Creek drainage. From the saddle, the southwest ridge is a rarity in the Grenadiers—a walkup. Be prepared not to be disappointed by the false summit at 13,392. The true summit is a rounded heap covered by boulders another quarter mile north.

Peak Three (13,478 feet)

NORTHWEST FACE — From the Vestal Creek drainage, use the same initial approach as discussed for Peak Two. Once on top at 12,800, the northwest face is a class two talus field.

EAST FACE — From the Trinity Creek drainage, hike up to the base of the east face which is composed of a large, stable talus field. Climb directly up the talus field to a false summit and then walk the ridge to the true summit.

Peak One (13,589 feet)

NORTHEAST RIDGE — Peak One is usually climbed in conjunction with White Dome from a camp at either Vallecito Lake or Eldorado Lake. The initial object is the 13,180-foot saddle between White Dome and Peak One. Once at the saddle, climb over point 13,401 to gain the easy northeast ridge.

White Dome (13,627 feet)

SOUTHWEST RIDGE — From the Peak One-White Dome saddle, the southeast ridge is a moderate scramble. With the exception of a few deviations to the left (west), stay right on the ridge.

Peak Seven (13,682 feet)

NORTH RIDGE — The north ridge is best approached by hiking up the Tenmile Creek drainage above Balsam Lake. Climb to the small lake between Peaks Eight and Seven. From the lake, climb up the talus field due west of the lake to gain the ridge at a high 13,020-foot saddle. From the saddle, stay on the ridge until you reach a gap in the ridge at 13,400 which requires you to make a tricky downclimb to the right (west). Once over the gap, it is an easy scramble to the top.

Peak Eight (13,228 feet)

WEST RIDGE — A six pitch, fifth class route over loose rock was reported in the July 1964 *Trail and Timberline*. The first pitch climbs forty feet to a ledge which traverses right to a forty-foot vertical crack. The crack leads to the skyline ridge. On the second pitch the difficulty eases and the quality of rock improves. The third pitch is a scramble. The fourth climbs "delicately up and left around a vertical tower." The first ascent party felt that the west ridge "with one possible exception" was "the easiest on the peak and it was none too easy."

NORTH FACE - EAST RIDGE — This route must be the "one possible exception" although it also involves some difficulty. The initial objective is to reach the notch east of the true summit, which separates Peak 8 from Point 13,100. One way to gain the notch is to start on the right (west) of the north face and work your way left (east) along alternating bands of rock and grass. The other way is an ice ax/crampon climb of the snow couloir which angles up to the notch from the east. Once at the notch, follow the east ridge to the top. The rock on the ridge is very loose and lichen covered. In wet conditions, it is dangerous. At several points, there is a significant amount of exposure on this narrow ridge.

Peak Nine (13,402 feet)

SOUTH FACE - SOUTHEAST RIDGE — From a camp south of Peak Nine in the Leviathan drainage, Art Tauchen climbed north toward the ridge between Peak Nine and Peak 13,176 and then began working northwest on a series of ledges covered with loose and unstable rock until reaching the summit. Tauchen feels that Peak Nine was the hardest peak on his trip into the eastern Grenadiers.

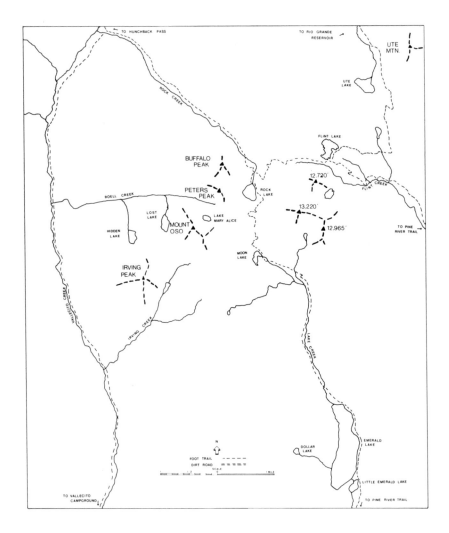

TO HUNCHBACK PASS

TO RIO GRANDE
RESERVOIR

UTE
MTN.

UTE
LAKE

ROCK CREEK

FLINT LAKE

BUFFALO
PEAK

PETERS
PEAK

ROELL CREEK

LOST
LAKE

HIDDEN
LAKE

MOUNT
OSO

LAKE
MARY ALICE

ROCK
LAKE

12,720'

13,220'

12,965'

FLINT CREEK

TO PINE
RIVER TRAIL

IRVING
PEAK

MOON
LAKE

VALLECITO CREEK

IRVING CREEK

LAKE CREEK

N

FOOT TRAIL ------
DIRT ROAD =====
SCALE

1 MILE

DOLLAR
LAKE

EMERALD
LAKE

TO VALLECITO
CAMPGROUND

LITTLE EMERALD LAKE

TO PINE RIVER TRAIL

RIO GRANDE PYRAMID — MOUNT OSO GROUP

The mountains between Vallecito Creek and the Pine River north of Vallecito Dam are a popular area for hikers, backpackers, and fishermen. There are also several peaks in the area of interest to climbers. When approached from the south by either the Pine or Vallecito trails, a two-day backpack is generally required to get into the heart of the area around Moon, Rock, and Flint lakes.

The highest peak in the area is Rio Grande Pyramid, located on the Continental Divide northeast of the main body of peaks. The highest peak in the main cluster is Mount Oso, which is centrally located among a group of high mountain lakes. To the south of Mount Oso lie Emerald Lake, Dollar Lake, and Moon Lake. At 279 acres, Emerald Lake is the second largest natural lake in Colorado. To the west of Mount Oso are Hidden Lake and Lost Lake which, as their names suggest, are both remote and hard to find. To the northeast lies Rock Lake, the Flint Lakes, and Ute Lake.

Rio Grande Pyramid and Mount Oso are the only high thirteeners in the area. There are, however, several low thirteeners and high 12,000-foot peaks in the area of interest. Irving Peak, which is located in the southwest area of the group, is a rugged pyramid which has caught the attention of many climbers by virtue of its prominent position at the head of Vallecito Creek when viewed from below. Several unnamed peaks just south of Flint Lakes make for enjoyable day hiking from a campsite at the lakes.

Ute Benchmark, located between Flint Lakes and Rio Grande Pyramid on the Continental Divide, is frequently climbed by backpackers crossing over the divide between the Rio Grande and San Juan drainages.

CLIMBING HISTORY

The first recorded ascent of a peak in the area was the Wheeler Survey's climb of Rio Grande Pyramid in 1874. Lieutenant William L. Marshall of the Wheeler Survey reported that the Rio

The Wheeler Survey team. A division of the Wheeler Survey made the first recorded ascent of Rio Grande Pyramid in 1874. George M. Wheeler is probably either the seventh from the left or sixth from the right. *Photo courtesy of USGS.*

Grande Pyramid is "one of the handsomest and most symmetrical cones in Colorado."[1] The Hayden Survey team arrived in the area shortly after the Wheeler Survey and was also impressed with the beauty of Rio Grande Pyramid. Rhoda reported that "its pyramidal form is almost perfect, while at the same time there is just enough bluff intermingled with the debris slopes to give relief without the usual accompaniment of coarseness."[2] Upon reaching the summit, the Hayden team found a "nicely built monument of stones" and speculated that "its builder was something other than a common miner."[3] They were right. In fact, the monument they found was the cairn left by the Wheeler Survey.

After climbing Rio Grande Pyramid, the Hayden team turned its attention to nearby Mount Oso, which they found to be "very steep and difficult to climb."[4] Just below the summit, the party was startled by a small grizzly bear which suddenly jumped up a few yards in front of them. The encounter prompted the Hayden team to name the peak "Mount Oso," which is the Spanish word for bear.

Notes

1. Bueler, *Roof of the Rockies*, p. 68.
2. Rhoda, *Summits to Reach*, pp. 47-48.
3. *Ibid.*, p. 51.
4. *Ibid.*, p. 52.

ACCESS AND HIKING

Vallecito Creek - Rock Creek

Vallecito Creek Trail along with the Pine River Trail is one of the most popular and well-traveled trails in the San Juans.

Vallecito Reservoir is located thirteen miles north of Bayfield (on U.S. 160) or twenty miles east of Durango on Florida Road. Once at the dam, stay west or left of the dam for five miles where you will come to a well-marked road junction which gives you a choice between Vallecito Campground and Pine River Campground. Turn left at the junction and drive three miles to Vallecito Campground and the trailhead.

The first mile of the trail climbs steeply and affords fine views of the spectacular Vallecito Creek gorge. The trail starts on the west side of Vallecito Creek and crosses over to the east on a bridge at three miles and then back to the west at slightly over five miles. At 6.5 miles, the trail crosses a third bridge. For the first three miles, you are likely to share the trail with many day hikers. After three miles, there are good campsites along the trail which never strays far from the river.

At mile fourteen, the Rock Creek Trail takes off to the east. From the junction of the Vallecito Creek and Rock Creek trails it is four miles up to Rock Lake and 5.5 miles to Flint Lakes. Flint Lakes is the more popular campsite since Rock Lake is above timberline. There are also some good campsites in the Rock Creek drainage before reaching timberline.

A good way to break up this two-day hike is to camp about nine miles up the Vallecito Creek Trail around the area where the Johnson Creek Trail takes off to the west. From this area, it is also possible to climb Irving Peak, which lies just to the east, 4,000 vertical feet above. Mount Oso can also be climbed from Vallecito Creek in a long day. Rock Creek is the best campsite if you are interested in climbing Mount Oso. A campsite at Flint Lakes provides a good base of operation for several day hikes of the unnamed peaks to the south or Ute Benchmark to the north. In addition, Rio Grande Pyramid can be climbed from a camp at Flint Lakes in a very long day.

Pine River, Lake Creek, Flint Creek Trails

To reach the trailhead for the Pine River Trail, proceed to the road junction north of Vallecito Reservoir, which is described above. From the road junction, stay to the right and travel a little over seven miles to the trailhead. The first six miles of the trail are relatively flat. After six miles you reach the trail up Lake Creek which turns to the left and climbs 1,600 vertical feet in four miles to Little Emerald Lake and Emerald Lake. Once at the lakes, the trail stays on the right side of the lake and continues to Moon Lake at 11,620 feet. The total distance from the Pine River Trail to Moon Lake is a little over nine miles. From Moon Lake, there is a rugged trail which climbs to the 12,420-foot pass connecting the Rock Creek and Lake Creek drainages.

The best way to reach Flint Lakes is to stay on the Pine River Trail rather than turning off on the Emerald Lake Trail. The turnoff to the Flint Creek Trail is located at mile twelve on the Pine River Trail. From the Pine, seven miles and a 2,400-foot elevation gain will bring you to Flint Lakes.

Thirty Mile Campground

The trail from Thirty Mile Campground provides the most direct access for a climb of Rio Grande Pyramid. The turnoff to Thirty Mile Campground is located on Colorado 149, twenty-four miles south of Lake City or nineteen miles west of Creede. From the turnoff, Thirty Mile Campground is eleven miles southwest, just below Rio Grande Reservoir. From the campground, the trail climbs west for 1.5 miles along Rio Grande Reservoir and then turns southwest and follows Weminuche Creek to the top of Weminuche Pass. Weminuche Pass connects the Rio Grande drainage with the Pine River drainage. From the pass, it is best to continue another mile south to the trail which climbs up the Rincon de la Vaca. Two miles up the Rincon de la Vaca Trail will put you at timberline and in good position to climb the eastern flank of Rio Grande Pyramid.

CLIMBING ROUTES

Rio Grande Pyramid (13,821 feet)

SOUTHWEST COULOIR — The southwest couloir is the most direct route when the peak is approached from the Flint Lake or Ute Lake area. The couloir is filled with talus and scree and hence, you will be tempted to exit the couloir to the right and try several class three scrambles which are possible on the south buttress.

EAST FACE — In *Colorado's Other Mountains*, Walter R. Borneman reports that from timberline in the Rincon de la Vaca drainage "route finding is a matter of choice. The most obvious option is to mount the hump of the Pyramid's east flank and then

Rio Grande Pyramid looking west from the upper Rincon de la Vaca drainage. *Photo by Walter R. Borneman.*

scamper up the northeast ridge another mile to the top. The summit ridge is steep and broken, but of generally stable volcanic rock."

Ute Benchmark (12,892 feet)

SOUTHEAST FACE — The climb up the southeast face is a grind. For every two steps you take forward, you will slide one step back. The main attraction to this climb is the descent. For those with sturdy knees and ankles, the romp downhill is a delight.

Mount Oso (13,684 feet)

SOUTHWEST RIDGE — Mount Oso can be combined with Irving Peak in a long day from the Vallecito. From the saddle north of Irving, drop down into the drainage north of Irving Lake and then climb up to the saddle between Peak 12,884 and Mount Oso. Haskell Rosebrough reports that the southwest ridge looks very difficult but is entirely negotiable. The most difficult portion of the climb is found near the summit where it is necessary to climb over some large rocks which appear unstable. The best descent route follows the southeast ridge down to the Irving Creek drainage, which leads you back to the Vallecito. In the lower portion of the drainage it is best to stay on the north side of the creek.

SOUTHEAST RIDGE — Mount Oso can be approached from either Rock Lake or Moon Lake. The initial objective is to reach the basin east of the false summit southeast of the true summit. From the basin, George Bell, Jr., chose a route which starts at the bottom of the main couloir coming down from the left (south) side of the false summit. After climbing 200 feet northwest up the gentle scree, a series of grass ledges appear on the left side of the slope. Follow the grass as it bends left up a gully, past a snow patch to the ridge, gaining it at 13,000 feet. Once on the ridge, it is an easy scramble over or around the false summit to the top.

Mount Oso from the summit of Irving Peak. *Photo by Haskell Rosebrough.*

Peak 12,740, "Flint Peak"
(One mile east of Rock Lake)

Flint Peak is the prominent peak which dominates the view south of Flint Lake. From Flint Lake, it is best climbed by hiking to the southernmost Flint Lake at 11,792 feet. From the lake, follow the southeast ridge.

Peak 12,965, "Mount Lobo"
(1 1/3 miles southeast of Rock Lake)

From the southernmost Flint Lake, climb to gain the low saddle on the eastern basin which surrounds the lake. Once at the saddle, it is an easy walk over broken rock to the summit.

Peak 13,220
(¾ mile southeast of Rock Lake)

Although it appears very rugged, the eastern flank of this peak is actually a very enjoyable scramble over good rock.

Irving Peak (13,218 feet)

WESTERN FACE - NORTH RIDGE — From a campsite one-quarter mile south of Johnson Creek, Haskell Rosebrough suggests aiming for the talus slope up to a saddle on the ridge north of Irving. From the saddle, there is easy access along the ridge to the summit of Irving. From the campsite, it is necessary to gain slightly over 4,000 vertical feet to reach the summit.

Approaching the summit of Redcloud Peak. *Photo by Ernie Stromeyer.*

LAKE CITY WEST GROUP

The Lake City West Group is a rather loosely defined group of high, rounded summits between Lake City and Silverton. The area is best known for its three fourteeners, Redcloud Peak, Sunshine Peak, and Handies Peak, which are, together with San Luis Peak, the easiest fourteeners in the San Juans to climb. Redcloud and Sunshine are located just north of the Lake Fork of the Gunnison River and are usually climbed together. Handies Peak is located just east of American Basin.

There has been renewed interest in the area since many climbers have completed the fourteeners and are now seeking to climb the hundred highest peaks in Colorado. In addition to the three fourteeners, there are six other peaks in the area which exceed 13,800 feet. Niagara Peak, Jones Mountain, and American Peak (13,806) lie south of American Basin and east of Burns Gulch and can be climbed in a day from either approach. Peaks 13,832 and 13,811 lie northeast of Redcloud Peak and are usually climbed in tandem from the trail up Silver Creek. Half Peak (13,841) lies to the south of the other peaks in the group and requires a long hiking approach.

In addition to the peaks exceeding 13,800, there are several high peaks just north of Cinnamon Pass of interest: Wood Mountain, Peak 13,708, and Peak 13,722.

CLIMBING HISTORY

The Lake City West Group was one of the areas of the San Juans in which miners probably preceded the surveyors to the top of several summits. The Hayden and Wheeler surveys sent parties into the area after the Brunot Treaty of September 13, 1873 granted the United States Government most of the San Juan Mountains which had been occupied previously by the Ute Indians. Even though the San Juans officially belonged to the Ute Indians, some miners had been prospecting in the area since the 1860s.

One of the peaks which was almost certainly climbed by miners was Handies Peak. The Hayden Survey team climbed Handies on August 14, 1874 and found the climb was a "very easy matter."[1] On the way up, they found some shallow prospect holes sunk in a vein at about 13,500.

Just before climbing Handies, Rhoda and Wilson of the Hayden team climbed Sunshine Peak and survived a near miss with lightning. Once on the summit, Rhoda reported feeling "a particular tickling sensation along the roots of our hair" and a "tickling sound" which increased until it sounded like the noise "produced by the frying of bacon."[2] After rapidly concluding their work on the summit, Rhoda and Wilson "had scarcely got more than thirty feet from the top when it was struck. We had only just missed it, and we felt thankful for our narrow escape."[3]

Before leaving the area, the Hayden party also climbed Peak 13,772 which "commands the headwaters of the Animas."[4]

The first reported ascent of Redcloud Peak was made by J.C. Spiller of the Wheeler Survey. Spiller also gave the peak its name because of its "brilliant red color, which continues nearly to its base."[5]

It appears that Niagara Peak and Jones Mountain received their names as hand-me-downs from Redcloud and Sunshine. In *14,000 Feet*, John L. Jerome Hart reports that Redcloud Peak was called Jones Peak in the 1890s and Sunshine Peak was called Niagara Peak.

An editorial note in the November 1935 *Trail and Timberline* gives an interesting insight into the frequency with which peaks in this region were climbed in the early days. In 1921 William F. Ervin, Carl Blaurock, and Dudley T. Smith left a CMC register on the summit of Handies. Fourteen years later in 1935, Kenneth Segerstrom of the USGS climbed Handies and reported that forty-one climbers in fifteen different parties had climbed Handies during the intervening years. Eight of the forty-one climbers had been women. It is probably safe to say that at least that many climbers now climb Handies on an average August weekend.

The rounded summits in this region do not afford climbers many opportunities for technical climbing. One exception is the rugged 800-foot north face of Half Peak which was climbed in May 1973 by Larry Derby and Jeff Lowe.[6]

Notes

1. Rhoda, *Summits to Reach*, p. 30.
2. *Ibid.*, p. 21.
3. *Ibid.*, pp. 24, 25.
4. *Ibid.*, p. 33.
5. Lieutenant W. L. Marshall, *Annual Report of the Wheeler Survey for 1876.*
6. 1973 *American Alpine Journal*, pp. 432-433.

ACCESS AND HIKING

Silver Creek Trail

Silver Creek Trail is the best means of access when climbing Sunshine Peak, Redcloud Peak, Peak 13,832, and Peak 13,811. To reach the trailhead, turn right off Colorado 149, 2.5 miles south of Lake City, and drive past Lake San Cristobal. Follow the Lake

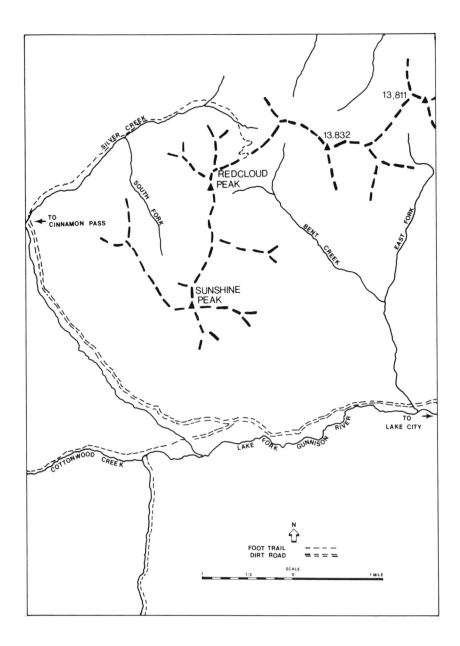

SILVER CREEK

TO CINNAMON PASS

SOUTH FORK

REDCLOUD PEAK

13,811

13,832

BENT CREEK

EAST FORK

SUNSHINE PEAK

TO LAKE CITY

LAKE FORK GUNNISON RIVER

COTTONWOOD CREEK

N

FOOT TRAIL
DIRT ROAD

SCALE
1   1/2   0   1 MILE

Fork of the Gunnison River on a well-maintained gravel road for a total of nineteen miles from Lake City where you reach the trailhead at 10,400-foot elevation. From the trailhead, hike 3.5 miles to the 13,020-foot pass northeast of Redcloud. From the pass, Redcloud and Sunshine lie to the southwest and Peaks 13,832 and 13,811 lie to the northeast. Roughly 1.7 miles up the trail you have the option of turning south on the trail up the south fork of Silver Creek, which will lead you to a cairn-marked route on the west side of Redcloud Peak.

Grizzly Gulch

From the same point on the road for the Silver Creek Trail, a trail heads in exactly the opposite direction (southwest) up Grizzly Gulch Creek. After two miles, you will reach timberline at approximately 12,000 feet. The summit of Handies is four miles from the trailhead.

Burns Gulch

Burns Gulch provides the best means of access for climbing Jones Mountain and Niagara Peak. In addition, it is possible to climb American Peak (13,806 feet) from Burns Gulch. The best way to reach Burns Gulch is to drive east from Silverton past Howardsville and Eureka. The turnoff for Burns Gulch is eleven miles from Silverton on an old mining road on the east side of the Animas. From the Animas, it is 2.5 miles and 2,500 vertical feet to the 13,220-foot saddle between Jones Mountain and Niagara Peak.

Grouse Gulch

The old abandoned mining road up Grouse Gulch is only .2 mile north of the Burns Gulch turnoff. When climbing Jones, Niagara, and American from the Animas, Grouse Gulch can be

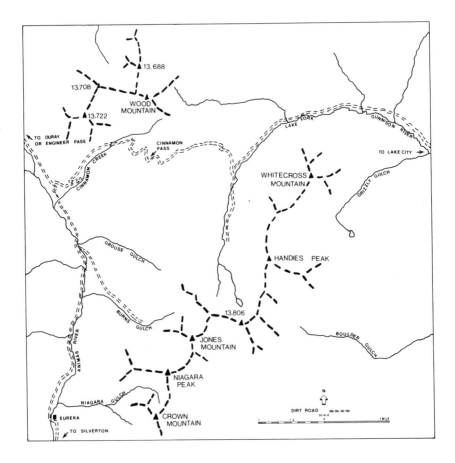

used as an alternate ascent or descent route to Burns Gulch. You climb 2,200 vertical feet over two miles to reach the 13,020-foot saddle which connects you with American Basin.

Cinnamon Pass

Cinnamon Pass is a 12,620-foot, four-wheel drive pass, fifteen miles northeast of Silverton. To reach Cinnamon Pass, drive past Howardsville and Eureka. After eleven miles, the road crosses over to the east side of the Animas. At mile 12.6 you will come to a sharp switchback to the right which you take toward the pass. Cinnamon Pass and the road that leads to it provide excellent access for Wood Mountain, Peak 13,708, and Peak 13,722. In addition, Cinnamon Pass provides access to Grizzly Gulch, Silver Creek Trail, and American Basin from the Silverton side.

American Basin

American Basin is located 3.5 miles southeast of Cinnamon Pass or a total of 18.5 miles from Silverton. It is also twenty-four miles from Lake City and five miles past the Silver Creek trailhead. Four-wheel drive is essential to get up into the upper portion of the basin. The basin provides excellent access for climbing Handies Peak and American Peak (13,806). In addition, it provides reasonable access to Jones Mountain and Niagara Peak. For those not interested in climbing the peaks, the hike to Sloan Lake at 12,900 feet is worthwhile. The rugged north faces of the peaks which line American Basin contrast sharply with the rounded summits which are the rule in this region.

Cataract Lake Trail

To reach the trailhead from Lake City, drive past Lake San Cristobal and up the Lake Fork of the Gunnison River. At mile fifteen, take a left and drive another mile to the ghost town site of Sherman. Continue across the Lake Fork on a bridge and go about one-third mile to the trailhead at 9,600 feet. From the trailhead, Rich Riefenberg reports that you wade Cottonwood Creek and hike a good trail south along Cataract Gulch. Although not shown on the USGS map, the trail switchbacks on the east side of the gulch earlier. Continue up the drainage past small ponds in the willow-filled meadows. For access to Half Peak, cross Cataract Creek at about 11,600 feet and climb southeast through willows to tundra. Then walk west and north on the 12,940 saddle northwest of the peak.

CLIMBING ROUTES

Redcloud Peak (14,034 feet)

NORTHEAST RIDGE — From the 13,020-foot pass on the northeast shoulder of Redcloud, the northeast ridge is an easy climb over loose, small scree.

NORTHWEST FACE — Once around to the north of Redcloud on the Silver Creek Trail, it is possible to climb the grassy slope on Redcloud's northwest flank. This route is more direct and also avoids some of the scree on the northeast ridge.

Sunshine Peak (14,001 feet)

NORTH RIDGE — Since most people climb Redcloud Peak and Sunshine together, the preferred route is to climb Redcloud Peak and then traverse south along the ridge to reach the summit of Sunshine Peak. When climbed in this manner, Sunshine Peak is a walk-up. Rather than hiking back over Redcloud Peak, it is better to return to the saddle between Sunshine Peak and Point

13,841. You can then descend steep, loose talus down to the south fork of Silver Creek which will lead you back to the Silver Creek Trail.

Peak 13,832
(1½ miles northeast of Redcloud Peak)

NORTHWEST RIDGE — From the 13,020-foot pass northeast of Redcloud, Rich Riefenberg suggests heading northeast on a broad ridge before traversing the north side of 13,561 on steep terrain. After the traverse, gain the northwest ridge where moderate chiprock leads you to the summit.

Peak 13,811
(2½ miles northeast of Redcloud Peak)

SOUTHWEST RIDGE — From the summit of Peak 13,832, Riefenberg advises descending east to the 13,500-foot saddle and then bypassing the 13,632-foot ridge point on the south side to gain the 13,260-foot saddle. The easy southwest ridge then leads to the summit.

Handies Peak (14,048 feet)

WEST FACE — From 12,000 feet in American Basin, you can choose just about any route you wish on the west face. The steep, grassy slopes on the lower portion of the west face eventually give way to loose scree higher on the mountain.

NORTH RIDGE — The north ridge is the best route on Handies when approached by the Grizzly Gulch Trail. From Grizzly Gulch aim for the low point between Handies Peak and Peak 13,577 to the north to avoid the cliffs on the east face of Handies and then follow the ridge directly to the summit.

Handies Peak (center), Whitecross Mountain (right), as viewed from the Silver Creek Trail. *Photo by Thomas S. Sawyer.*

Niagara Peak (13,807 feet)

NORTHWEST RIDGE — The northwest ridge starts at the 13,220-foot saddle betwen Jones and Niagara which is best gained from Burns Gulch. From the saddle, Rich Riefenberg describes the ridge as being "straightforward."

Jones Mountain (13,860 feet)

NORTHEAST RIDGE — From the 13,140-foot saddle northeast of Jones, Riefenberg describes the northeast ridge as "a short, steepish pull on generally stable terrain."

Peak 13,806, "American Peak"
(1 mile southwest of Handies Peak)

WEST RIDGE — To reach the west ridge, it is necessary to do some ridge walking after approaching from either American Basin, Grouse Gulch, or Burns Gulch. Before reaching the summit, Riefenberg reports that you will encounter some minor ups and downs, together with some unstable talus.

American Peak (left), Niagara Peak, and Jones Mountain (right) from the summit of Handies Peak. Sloan Lake is in the center foreground. *Photo by Jay Mason.*

Wood Mountain (13,660 feet approx.)

SOUTH FACE - WEST RIDGE — From the top of Cinnamon Pass, Haskell Rosebrough reports that an old mining road contouring up the south face is an attractive way to reach the saddle to the left (west) of the peak. From the saddle you can follow the west ridge, which presents no problem, to the summit. From Cinnamon Pass the climb to the summit is only slightly over 1,000 vertical feet.

Peak 13,708
(¾ mile northwest of Wood Mountain)

SOUTHEAST RIDGE — Peak 13,708 does not quite meet the 300 vertical feet requirement used by many to define a peak. It is only a few feet shy. Nevertheless, it does combine well with Wood Mountain and Peak 13,722 and for that reason is described here. From Wood Mountain, Haskell Rosebrough walked the southeast ridge without difficulty.

Peak 13,722
(1 mile southwest of Wood Mountain)

NORTHEAST RIDGE — From the summit of 13,708 you use the ridge between the two peaks to climb 13,722. Haskell Rosebrough described the ridge as being on flat and stable rock. Although not particularly difficult, it does keep your interest. The last part of the climb is on steep, sandy talus.

SOUTHEAST FACE — From the flat area around 12,200 feet on the Cinnamon Pass road, you can pick your route up the grassy slopes of the southeast face.

Half Peak (13,841 feet)

NORTHEAST RIDGE — From the Cataract Gulch drainage shoot to gain the 12,940-foot saddle northeast of the summit. From the saddle, Rich Riefenberg reports that you climb a steep talus ridge southeast, then over the ridge into steep, loose gullies. You will come to a short exposed section of third class climbing and then a flat walk west to the summit.

NORTH FACE— After an approach from Square Gulch in May, the 1973 *American Alpine Journal* reports that the first ascent party scrambled up the lower face via the third class rounded buttress in the right center of the face and climbed a snow arete to the first steep cliff band. They followed a snow ramp to the right for two pitches to the ledge separating the upper from the lower cliff band. They then climbed directly above on a sometimes rotten prow to the flat summit. The route is rated NCCS III, F8.

UNCOMPAHGRE GROUP

Contrasts typify the Uncompahgre Group. Difficult climbs are located adjacent to walkups. The area's two fourteeners are a case in point. While Uncompahgre Peak is one of the easier fourteeners to climb, nearby Wetterhorn is one of the more difficult. Coxcomb and Redcliff are another example. Coxcomb is by anyone's standards a difficult climb. Redcliff, located immediately north, is a walkup.

Many difficult climbs can be found interspersed through the area. Technical routes have been established on the north faces of Wetterhorn, Coxcomb, and Wildhorse peaks and the south face of Chimney Rock. Like Wetterhorn and Coxcomb, Heisshorn and El Punto are challenging even by their easiest route. On the other hand, Matterhorn, Wildhorse, Courthouse, and Fortress are easy to moderate climbs.

The group is best approached from two entirely different directions. The southern peaks, such as Uncompahgre, Wetterhorn, Matterhorn, and Wildhorse are best approached from the south and east (Lake City). The northeast peaks are more accessible when approached from the north or west (Montrose or Ridgway). Virtually all of the peaks in the area are day hikes.

Another aspect of the area which deserves note are the wild rock formations in the northern area. Rotten pinnacles near Dunsinane and Precipice peaks and the nearby ridges sometimes give you a feeling that you are in another world.

CLIMBING HISTORY

Uncompahgre Peak was probably climbed by Indians before the arrival of the surveyors. The San Juan Mountaineers reported that there was "direct evidence" that Indians had "carried their hunting expeditions at least to an elevation of 13,000 feet on the peak."[1]

Uncompahgre Peak is one of several peaks in the San Juans on which the Wheeler and Hayden surveys overlapped territory. The Hayden team climbed Uncompahgre on August 8, 1874. Although they were "expecting to have a very difficult climb," the Hayden team "found the ascent very easy."[2] Although the Hayden team did not encounter technical difficulties, they "were terribly taken aback, however, when, at an elevation of over 13,000 feet, a she grizzly, with her two cubs, came rushing past them from the top of the peak."[3]

The Wheeler Survey, which also climbed Uncompahgre Peak in 1874, reported an even closer encounter with "a large cinnamon bear and her cub" which they found "sportively tumbling and rolling from the summit."[4] One of the packers from the Wheeler team was raising his head above a ledge when "the bear happened to be about to look down over the same place." Although both the bear and the packer "tumbled off the cliff together," the packer escaped with only "a good fright and a few bruises."

The only other climb reported during the 1800s was the August 25, 1899 climb of Wildhorse Peak which lies several miles southwest of Wetterhorn Peak overlooking American Flats from the north. Wildhorse Peak was climbed by Eli Stanton, F.H. Stanton, and William Killen. The climb was part of a trout fishing trip in which Eli Stanton wished to give his visiting relatives "a

W.H. Jackson's photo of Uncompahgre Peak taken during the 1870s. *Courtesy U.S. Geological Survey.*

thrill."[5] Although the exact route was not reported, they apparently took a route with some exposure, as F.H. Stanton "was forced, through nervousness, to crawl on his hands and knees."[6]

Wetterhorn Peak was climbed in 1906 by George C. Barnard, Reverend David Utter, Will P. Smedley, and Clyde Smedley, who set out with plans to climb Uncompahgre Peak. While passing by the base of Wetterhorn it became "evident to everyone that we were passing a peak that was worthy of our metal, both in difficulty and in height." This party, which climbed Wetterhorn by what is now the standard route of the south ridge, remarked as to the feeling of "half exhiliration and half fear which was created by the 600 ft. exposure of the last pitch."[7]

Another early climb of Wetterhorn was made on August 8, 1920 by Albert Ellingwood and Barton Hoag, who made the first ascent of the peak's east ridge. Uncompahgre was the last peak in the San Juans climbed by William S. Cooper and John Hubbard during their 1908 excursion. Cooper reported that "Uncompahgre is a magnificent mountain, but disappointingly easy. A friend of mine, approaching it from a different direction from ours, climbed to within 700 feet of its summit on his motorcycle."[8]

Several first ascents were made in the area during the 1929 summer outing of the Colorado Mountain Club. Two of the peaks climbed during the outing are unnamed on topographical maps. They are the Heisshorn, which lies one mile directly north of Wetterhorn Peak at 13,411 feet, and El Punto, which lies a little under two miles north of Matterhorn Peak at 13,280 feet. Both peaks were climbed by Dwight Lavender and Forrest Greenfield, who reported that even though El Punto "looked like an unconquerable pillar of stone," actually the Heisshorn was the more difficult climb of the two and was probably the most difficult of the outing, "second only to Coxcomb."[9]

During the outing, Lavender and Greenfield set out to reconnoiter a route on Coxcomb. They did in fact find a way up the summit block of Coxcomb by a chimney on the southwest side. They were stopped just short of the summit by a thirty-foot vertical gap in the summit block. They did not have a rope with them and were forced to give up the climb at that point. Two days later a party of seven led by Henry Buchtel made the first complete ascent of Coxcomb. The first ascent party learned of the gap in the summit block from Lavender and Greenfield and, therefore, came prepared with a rope which they used to overcome the problem.

Chimney Rock and Lizard Head have commonly been held to be the most difficult peaks in Colorado to climb. There are differing opinions, however, as to which is the more difficult. Chimney Rock, which lies north of Courthouse Mountain and Coxcomb Peak on the westernmost ridge in the area, was first climbed on September 15, 1934 by Melvin Griffiths and Robert Ormes. The report of the first ascent in the February 1935 *Trail and Timberline* concluded that Chimney Rock was a "much more difficult climb than Lizard Head" but is a safer climb

Robert Ormes (left) and Mel Griffiths on the summit of Chimney Rock during the first ascent on September 15, 1934. *Photograph by Mel Griffiths.*

because it is "composed of well cemented conglomorate."[10] The initial report probably exaggerated the difficulty of Chimney Rock. Ormes, who also made an early ascent of Lizard Head, feels that Chimney Rock "couldn't be said, even in those days, to be difficult."[11] Ormes and Griffiths climbed the pinnacle "via a chimney and crack which splits the south face of the rock."[12]

New routes were not reported in the area until the 1960s when the north face of Coxcomb and the northeast face of Wildhorse Peak were climbed. The north face of Coxcomb Peak was climbed in August 1965 during a CMC outing by Dick Yeatts, Mike Stults, Dick Guadagno, and Martin Etter. The northeast face of Wildhorse Peak was climbed in August 1968 by Etter, John McDermott, Henry Barker, and Greg Simmons.

The 800-foot vertical north face of Wetterhorn which gives the peak its striking profile had been the subject of speculation for several decades. The first ascent of the north face was finally made in late September 1973 by Jeff Lowe and Paul Hogan. Lowe reported that they finished this difficult climb "in a snowstorm that added an alpine quality to the climb."[13]

Some of the first winter climbing in the San Juans took place in the area in 1934. Gordon Williams and Melvin Griffiths skied from the SJM shelter cabin in Blaine Basin to Ouray. From Ouray, they skied to Engineer Pass and climbed Engineer Mountain. After climbing Engineer Mountain, they skied across American Flats and climbed Wildhorse Peak. Later they established camp on the north fork of Henson Creek in the hope of making an ascent of Wetterhorn. After weathering a furious storm, Griffiths and Williams climbed Dolly Varden Mountain instead and then skied into Silverton to conclude their journey.[14]

Notes

1. *SJM Guide*, p. 84.

2. Rhoda, *Summits to Reach*, p. 15.

3. *Ibid.*

4. *Executive & Descriptive Report of Lt. William L. Marshall, Corps of Engineers, on the Operation of Party No. 1, Colorado Section; Field Season of 1875*, p. 95.

5. *T&T*, September 1942, p. 122.

6. *Ibid.*

7. *T&T*, August 1929, p. 6.

8. William S. Cooper, Unpublished Manuscript entitled "Mountains," p. 91.

9. *T&T*, October 1929, p. 6.

10. *T&T*, February 1935, p. 17.

11. Robert M. Ormes, Personal Correspondence.

12. *T&T*, February 1935, p. 17.

13. *American Alpine Journal*, 1975, p. 139.

14. *T&T*, February 1935.

ACCESS AND HIKING

Nellie Creek

From downtown Lake City, take the gravel road which heads west up Henson Creek. The turnoff from Lake City is marked by a sign which directs you toward Engineer Pass. At four miles you will pass through Henson and at 5.5 miles you will reach the Nellie Creek turnoff. At the junction of Nellie and Henson creeks, a jeep trail heads north up the Nellie Creek drainage. From the creek junction, it is seven miles to the summit of Uncompahgre. If you have a four-wheel drive, it is possible to drive four miles to a trailhead close to timberline at 11,700 feet. Keep a close lookout for a sharp switchback to the left which you take at 2.5 miles. From the trailhead, a trail heads west toward Uncompahgre while another trail heads north over a 12,360-foot pass to Big Blue Creek. The Nellie Creek jeep trail is the best approach for climbing Uncompahgre alone.

Matterhorn Creek

To reach Matterhorn Creek, take the same gravel road up Henson Creek which leads you past the Nellie Creek turnoff to the North Henson Road, located 9.5 miles west of Lake City. Take a righthand turn and continue 2.1 miles up the drainage of the north fork of Henson Creek to the Ridge Stock Driveway Trail. It is possible to continue almost a mile up Matterhorn Creek drainage on this jeep trail until you are blocked at a metal gate at the boundary of the Uncompahgre Primitive Area. From the trailhead, you can hike up an old jeep trail to reach timberline in the basin southeast of Wetterhorn Peak and south of Matterhorn Creek. Matterhorn Creek is the best means of access for climbing Matterhorn and Wetterhorn. It is also the best approach if you wish to climb Wetterhorn and Uncompahgre in a long day.

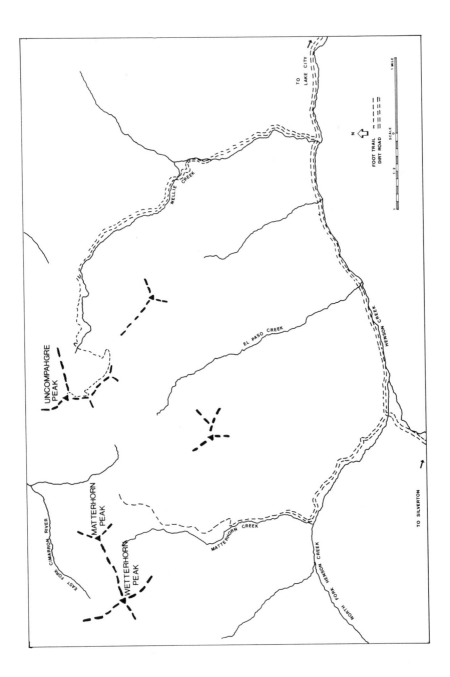

Engineer Pass - American Flats

Uncompahgre and Wetterhorn are most frequently approached from Lake City. It is possible, however, to approach from Silverton or Ouray by four-wheel drive over Engineer Pass. From Silverton, follow the road up the Animas River past Howardsville, Eureka, and Animas Forks to reach Engineer Pass. From Ouray, the turnoff to Engineer Pass is a little over three miles south of Ouray. Once at Engineer Pass, the road takes you east to American Flats with Wildhorse Peak to the north. From American Flats you then drop down into Henson Creek and pass through Capital City and Henson before reaching Lake City.

West Fork of the Cimmarron Road

The turnoff for this long but well-maintained gravel road is located 2.7 miles east of Cimmarron (Cimmarron is twenty miles east of Montrose) on U.S. 50. From the U.S. 50 turnoff, drive past the turnoffs to the Silver Jack Reservoir before reaching the roads to the East Fork of the Cimmarron at 20.3 miles and the Middle Fork at 20.5 miles. Bear right at both road junctions and continue past the turnoff to Owl Creek Pass at 27.1 miles until you cross the stream at thirty miles and reach the trailhead at 30.6 miles. To negotiate the last couple of miles and to cross the stream, a four-wheel drive or high clearance vehicle helps. From the trailhead, it is 2.5 miles and 1,800 vertical feet to the 12,500-foot pass which connects you with Wetterhorn Basin. The approaches for Coxcomb Peak, Redcliff, and Fortress all start on the West Fork Trail. Precipice, Dunsinance, Courthouse, and Chimney are all climbed from various points on the road north of the trailhead.

Owl Creek Pass Road

The Owl Creek Pass Road has been recently reopened after being closed for a couple of years by a landslide. When open, the

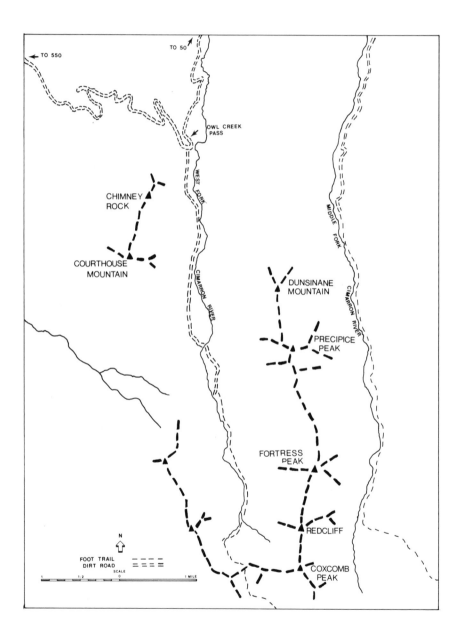

TO 550

TO 50

OWL CREEK PASS

WEST FORK

CIMARRON RIVER

MIDDLE FORK

CIMARRON RIVER

CHIMNEY ROCK

COURTHOUSE MOUNTAIN

DUNSINANE MOUNTAIN

PRECIPICE PEAK

FORTRESS PEAK

REDCLIFF

COXCOMB PEAK

N

FOOT TRAIL
DIRT ROAD

SCALE

1   1/2   0   1 MILE

road provides access to the West, Middle, and East forks of the Cimmarron from U.S. 550, 1.8 miles north of Ridgway. From U.S. 550, it is approximately thirteen miles east to the intersection with the West Fork of the Cimmarron road.

CLIMBING ROUTES

Uncompahgre Peak (14,309 feet)

SOUTH RIDGE— The south ridge of Uncompahgre Peak is the standard route. When Uncompahgre is approached from Nellie Creek, you can either follow the trail which contours around the basin southeast of Uncompahgre or head due west to gain the ridge at 13,800 feet, just north of the prominent notch. Once at 13,800 feet, the trail skirts the ridge to the west and requires you to scramble in a couple of spots before you reach the broad summit plateau. On the summit, you will note several stone windbreaks which have been constructed by overnight campers.

Cy Dixon climbing Uncompahgre Peak in December 1983. *Photo by Thomas S. Sawyer.*

SOUTHEAST FACE — A prominent band of cliffs runs along the southeast face at approximately 13,800 feet. It is possible to climb this band of cliffs by several routes which vary in difficulty but which all involve problems with loose rock. While at least one of the routes toward the western end of the cliff can be climbed third class, as a general rule you will want a rope, hard hat, and protection.

Wetterhorn Peak (14,015 feet)

SOUTHEAST RIDGE AND SOUTHWEST FACE — By its standard route, Wetterhorn is one of the more challenging fourteeners in the San Juans. The standard route contours up the eastern side of the southeast ridge until near the summit where you reach a keyhole separating the summit from a southern pinnacle. The last 150 feet of the southwest face, which is

Ike Weaver and Dan Neifert below Wetterhorn Peak. *Photo by Ernie Stromeyer.*

reached by passing through the keyhole, is what you will remember about this climb. The last 150 feet are made up of small ledges which are sprinkled by a covering of loose gravel. What makes the section exciting are the 600 feet of exposure. Early in the year when there is a chance of encountering snow and ice or in poor weather conditions a rope is comforting on this last section.

NORTH FACE — A report in the 1975 *American Alpine Journal* reports a climb up the "natural break in the middle" of the north face as being NCCS III, F7. The report also notes that "the 800-foot face required six leads and five hours."

Matterhorn Peak (13,590 feet)

SOUTH FACE — The lower portion of the south face consists of a grassy slope which you hike up directly toward the summit. As you near the summit, you will encounter some easy scrambling.

Wildhorse Peak (13,266 feet)

SOUTHWEST FACE — The October 1959 *Trail and Timberline* reports that Wildhorse "is easily climbed via a steep grassy slope from the southwest."

NORTHEAST FACE — The October 1969 *Trail and Timberline* reports a climb on the left side of the face consisting of three plus leads on the prominent corner of the face. The route was rated 5.6.

Coxcomb Peak (13,656 feet)

SOUTHWEST CHIMNEY — The approach to this route is roundabout at best. From the end of the road up the West Fork of the Cimmarron, hike up the trail to reach the 12,500-foot pass

Approaching the southwest chimney of Coxcomb Peak. The route on the summit block starts just above the climber's head. *Photo by Robert F. Rosebrough.*

one-half mile west of Coxcomb. Once at the pass, you have a choice between a high, rotten traverse or dropping down the trail to 12,100 feet and climbing up the basin southwest of Coxcomb. I think you will find that it saves time to avoid the traverse.

Once at the base of the summit block on the southwest end, you will find a twelve-foot vertical chimney by which you gain the easier middle section of the summit block. The last eighty feet are comprised of a sloping chimney. Most climbers will want a belay on both the first and last portions of the chimney. The middle section is an easy scramble. Once on top of the summit block, head northeast toward the summit until you are stopped by a thirty-foot gap.

The best way to negotiate the gap is for one climber at a time to be belayed down the gap and then back up after scrambling out to the true summit and signing the register. Negotiating the gap is the most difficult portion of the climb and definitely requires a rope belay.

On the downclimb, most climbers rappel the very top portion of the chimney and then downclimb the rest. The chimney is unusual in that, with the exception of the very top, it seems easier to downclimb than to ascend.

NORTH FACE — The October 1969 *Trail and Timberline* reports a route which "ascends snowbands and cliffs to a point 50 feet east of summit." The route was rated 5.3 and involves one or two leads.

Coxcomb Peak as viewed from the summit of Redcliff. Note the gap in the summit block which must be climbed to reach the true summit on the left. *Photo by Robert F. Rosebrough.*

Redcliff (13,642 feet)

SOUTH FACE — The 13,140-foot saddle between Redcliff and Coxcomb can be reached from either the West or Middle Fork of Cimmarron. Once at the saddle, the south face is an easy walkup over stable talus.

Peak 13,241, "Fortress Peak"
(½ mile north of Redcliff)

SOUTHWEST FACE — Tim Duffy reports that the southwest slopes of Fortress are a class two climb. Fortunately, the detached pinnacle you see from the summit is not quite the high point.

Precipice Peak (13,144 feet)

SOUTH RIDGE — From the West Fork trailhead, head east and slightly north to gain the south ridge which you then follow to the top. Duffy notes that there are no real difficulties on the climb. The climb is of particular interest because of the unusual rock formations north and east of the summit area.

Dunsinane Mountain (12,742 feet)

WEST FACE - NORTH RIDGE — To begin this climb, Tim Duffy suggests parking directly west of the summit about 1.4 miles south of the turnoff to Owl Creek Pass. After crossing the river, bushwack your way through the forest. The forest is slow, with log-jams, downed branches, and underbrush that can't be avoided. Aim for the north ridge near the prominent rock formations. There is a little scrambling at minor cliff bands near the top.

Courthouse Mountain (12,152 feet)

EAST RIDGE — A good place to begin a climb of Courthouse is 1.3 miles south of the Owl Creek turnoff on the West Fork road. From the road, Duffy reports that the east ridge is steep, short, and direct. The forest gives way to interesting and steep bands of grass and rock near the summit. From the summit you have excellent views of Chimney Peak to the north and Dunsinane and Precipice to the east.

Chimney Rock (11,781 feet)

SOUTH FACE — The February 1935 issue of *Trail and Timberline* reported that the first ascent was made "via a chimney and crack which splits the south face of the rock." The first ascent party "reached the foot of the crack after scrambling over a troublesome band of rock by means of [shoulder stands]. The vertical crack is some 400 feet in length and contains several interesting chockstones."

Peak 13,300, "El Punto"
(1¾ miles north of Matterhorn)

SOUTHWEST CHIMNEY — The report of the first ascent of El Punto contained in the October 1929 issue of *Trail and Timberline* described the peak as looking "like an unconquerable pillar of stone, but as we drew nearer, small chimneys and broken places began to take form." After rounding the southwest side of the mountain, the first ascent team found "a chimney leading to the bench which was almost half way up the peak. This point was gained without any difficulty. The rest of the way to the top was covered by scaling a series of small cliffs which were made possible by the numerous hand and foot holds." The shortest approach to El Punto would probably be the Middle Fork Trail.

Peak 13,411, "Heisshorn"
(1¼ miles north of Wetterhorn)

NORTHEAST RIDGE — The first ascent of Heisshorn is also described in the October 1929 *Trail and Timberline*. The first ascent party "worked [their] way along a knife edge ridge, but something worse was yet to come. The only possible way of gaining the summit was by scaling a cliff some fifty feet high. This wall was composed of loose rock which made climbing not only difficult, but dangerous." The report concluded by noting that "as a difficult climb Heisshorn remains in our memories of this outing second only to Coxcomb."

Bill Ervin, Carl Blaurock, and Dudley Smith atop San Luis Peak, 1921. *Photo courtesy of Carl Blaurock.*

SAN LUIS GROUP

High rounded summits with grassy slopes and long hiking approaches typify the San Luis group. The main group of peaks, of which San Luis Peak at 14,014 is the highest, is located directly north of Creede. In addition to San Luis, Stewart Peak, which is only seventeen feet shy of being a fourteener, Balto Alto, Organ Mountain, and Baldy Chato comprise the main group.

There is not a short way to approach these climbs. The quickest trips can be made from the east via the trails in the Nutras, Stewart, and Cochetopa Creek drainages, but each involves at least several miles of hiking before reaching the base of the peaks. Longer approaches are also available by means of West Willow Creek to the south and the Bondholder Trail to the northwest.

A somewhat separate group of peaks lies northeast of Creede. Creede Crest (13,895) and La Garita Benchmark (13,718) are the highest peaks in this group which can be approached from Creede by either the Inspiration Point Trail or East Willow Creek and the La Garita Stock Driveway.

CLIMBING HISTORY

Other than the survey climbs, very little is known about the early climbing history in the San Luis group. Stewart Peak was one of the first recorded ascents in the San Juans. It was climbed in 1873 by the Hayden Survey team. Frederick Endlich made the climb according to his field notebook, but it is not clear which of the other members of the division for that year, which included A.D. Wilson, George B. Chittenden, and Franklin Rhoda, made the climb. As late as 1965, Stewart Peak was considered to be a fourteener. The April 1965 *Trail and Timberline* reported that "the current USGS elevation listing shows Stewart Peak as 14,060 with a footnote indicating that the latest survey observation (U.S. Coast and Geodetic Survey) gives an elevation of 13,983." *Trail and Timberline* further reported that "further investigation indicates that no one knows where 14,060 came from, although CMC is listed as the source. CMC's elevation is 14,032, based on Hayden Survey figures." New vertical angle measurements taken by USGS resulted in the publication of an official elevation for Stewart Peak of 13,982 feet. Apparently that figure was also modified slightly since the current USGS quad map lists Stewart at 13,983.

The demotion of Stewart Peak left San Luis Peak as the only fourteener in the group. It is not known who made the first ascent of San Luis Peak. Presumably that feat was accomplished by miners. It was assumed for many years that the Hayden Survey team's Station 2 for 1874 was San Luis. While researching *Summits to Reach*, an annotated edition of Franklin Rhoda's *Report on the Topography of the San Juan Country*, Mike Foster established that Station 2 was actually Peak 13,502, two miles northeast of Baldy Cinco. There are no reports on the first ascents of other peaks in the area.

ACCESS AND HIKING

Stewart Creek

A long drive over a maze of dirt roads is a prerequisite to reach the Stewart Creek trailhead. The initial turnoff is located on Colorado 112, twenty miles south of U.S. 50 and forty-three miles northwest of Saguache. The road is marked as "Road NN 14." Follow this road for 7.2 miles to a junction where you turn right on what is designated as the Cochetopa Road and "Road 15 GG." Take a right at 11.3 ("Cochetopa Road") and 11.6 miles ("Road 15 GG") and then lefts at an unmarked junction at 15.4 miles and the junction with the Big Meadows Road at mile twenty-four. You cross Chavez Creek at mile twenty-five, Nutras Creek at mile 26.4, and reach the Stewart Creek trailhead at mile 28.6. The Stewart Creek drainage is completely filled with beaver ponds and hence the well-maintained trail stays on the right (north) side of the drainage on the wooded slope. From the trailhead, it is four miles and 1,500 vertical feet to timberline at 12,000 feet. The Stewart Creek Trail provides excellent access for Organ Mountain, San Luis Peak, and Baldy Alto.

Nutras Creek

Nutras Creek is reached at mile 26.4 on the dirt road approach to Stewart Creek. Initially you can either drive (four-wheel drive) or hike up the jeep road on the right (north) side of the drainage until the road gives out and you make your way via an assortment of sketchy trails. From the main dirt road it is four miles and 1,600 vertical feet to the 12,600-foot basin between Stewart Peak and Baldy Alto. Nutras Creek is the best approach for Stewart Peak and Peak 13,795. It is also a good approach for Baldy Alto. Although rather roundabout, Baldy Chato can also be climbed from Nutras Creek.

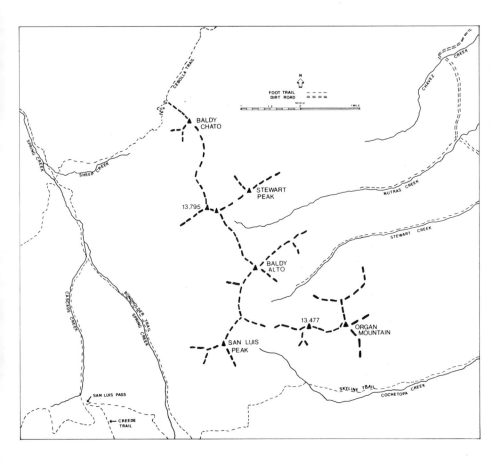

Cochetopa Creek - Skyline Trail

On its eastern end, the Skyline Trail follows the Cochetopa Creek drainage. The trailhead is .5 mile east of the Stewart Creek trailhead. The trail starts at a fence gate and skirts private property initially. From this trailhead, it is seven miles and 1,700 vertical feet to timberline in the basin southeast of San Luis Peak. San Luis Peak and Organ Mountain can both be climbed from this trail. It is, however, shorter to approach both from the Stewart Creek Trail.

Spring Creek - Bondholder Trail

The Bondholder Trail in the Spring Creek drainage approaches San Luis from the northwest. The trail is too long for a one-day climb of San Luis but does make for a nice backpack. To reach the trailhead, turn off Colorado 149, ten miles southeast of Lake City, and head northeast on dirt roads. Take the right fork at junctions at miles 15.7 and 16.8 to reach the trailhead. It is necessary to cross private property before reaching the National Forest boundary. From the trailhead it is six miles and 1,300 vertical feet to Bondholder Meadows at 10,400 where campsites are available.

Cebolla Trail

The east end of the Cebolla Trail which is described here can be used as a northern approach for Baldy Chato. Although the approach by road to the trailhead is accurately depicted on the Gunnison Forest Service map, the USGS quad (Stewart Peak) which was last revised in 1965 is inaccurate. The trailhead is located where the road crosses East Los Pinos Creek and can be reached from either the east or west. From the west it is twenty-nine miles from the Colorado 149 turnoff ten miles southeast of Lake City. From the east it is thirty-two miles from the Colorado 112 turnoff twenty miles south of U.S. 50. From the trailhead at 11,400 the trail climbs to 12,500 in two miles to the northwestern

flank of Baldy Chato before following the Sheep Creek drainage
down to Spring Creek.

Inspiration Point Trail

Rich Riefenberg reports that the Inspiration Point Trail can be
used as access for climbing Creede Crest and La Garita
Benchmark. Although very long, it is a "most enjoyable climb on
very easy terrain." The trailhead is located on the east side of
Creede behind some buildings at 8,800 feet. Initially you hike the
steep trail north, then northeast through aspen, to Inspiration
Point. You then continue northeast across large aspen meadows
to the base of La Garita Benchmark. It is seven miles and 3,600
vertical feet to the base of the mountain.

East Willow Creek -
La Garita Stockdrive

In *Colorado's High Thirteeners,* Garratt and Martin describe a
shorter approach for Creede Crest and La Garita Benchmark,
which follows the road and trail up East Willow Creek north of
Creede and then turns right (east) to follow the La Garita Stock
Driveway to timberline.

CLIMBING ROUTES

San Luis Peak (14,014 feet)

NORTHEAST RIDGE — From Stewart Creek the large face you
see at the head of the drainage is not the summit of San Luis. It is
the northeastern flank. Although just about any way will go, the

San Luis Peak after a mid-September snow. The summit is the rounded point at the end of the long ridge left of center. *Photo by Robert F. Rosebrough*.

fastest is probably to aim for the 13,175-foot saddle left (east) of the northeastern flank. Climb straight up the eastern ridge of the flank to the top and then follow the northeast ridge to the summit. There is a trail of sorts which you can follow to bypass one of the ridge points to the left (east). This climb, as are almost all the others in the area, is a walkup.

Organ Mountain (13,799 feet)

NORTHWEST RIDGE — After reaching timberline in the Stewart Creek drainage, continue upstream for about .3 mile before contouring to the northwest ridge. Initially, follow the ridge directly until you can begin traversing to the right (south) toward the saddle just north of the summit. The last two hundred feet are on talus. The rest of the climb is grassy slopes.

Organ Mountain. *Photo by Robert F. Rosebrough.*

Baldy Alto (13,698 feet)

SOUTHWEST RIDGE — From the saddle between San Luis and Baldy Alto, you can follow the ridge directly to the summit.

SOUTHEAST RIDGE — From timberline in Stewart Creek, the best route for Baldy Alto alone is to climb directly up the ridge dropping down to the southeast from the summit.

Stewart Peak (13,983 feet)

SOUTHEAST FACE — From the Nutras Creek drainage you can't go wrong as long as you are headed up. The entire southeast face is a gentle, grassy slope.

Peak 13,795
(1 mile southwest of Stewart Peak)

Peak 13,795 is the twin-summit peak southeast of Stewart Peak. Both summits can be climbed from the saddle between 13,795 and Stewart. There is only about 250 vertical elevation gain from the saddle to the western summit.

Peak 13,477
(1 mile west of Organ Mountain)

WEST RIDGE — From the saddle between San Luis and 13,477, traverse left (north) to avoid the cliffs on the point just west of 13,477 before gaining the ridge higher up and following it to the summit.

EAST RIDGE — There is a large, prominent gap which prevents you from ridge walking between Organ and 13,477. From Organ it is necessary to drop to the left (south) about 250 vertical feet on a rotten, difficult downclimb before climbing back up the ridge once the gap is passed.

Baldy Chato (13,401 feet)

SOUTH RIDGE — Although it is a long, somewhat roundabout approach, Baldy Chato can be climbed from Nutras Creek by the gentle south ridge. From the saddle between Stewart and 13,795, you actually lose more elevation than you gain to reach the summit. You drop about 350 feet to the level ridge and only regain 200 feet of it on the climb to the summit.

NORTHWEST FACE — It would appear that the best route for Baldy Chato alone would be to leave the Cebolla Trail as it begins to drop down into Sheep Creek and climb up the northwest face.

La Garita Benchmark (13,718 feet)

SOUTHWEST FACE — Rich Riefenberg reports that the southwest face is an easy climb over stable talus and boulders.

Peak 13,895, "Creede Crest"
(2 miles northwest of La Garita Benchmark)

SOUTHEAST RIDGE — From La Garita Benchmark, Riefenberg reports that you can follow the ridge directly to the summit on good terrain. If you are climbing Creede Crest alone, shoot to gain the ridge at the 13,580-foot saddle just southeast of the summit.

Ace Kvale leading the first ascent of Powder in the Sky (II, 5.10b) on the upper east buttress of Ophir Wall. *Photo courtesy of Antoine Savelli.*

ROCK CLIMBING IN THE SAN JUANS

In the 1970s, climbers in the San Juans began to develop several rock climbing areas. Although technical climbing in an alpine setting has taken place for many years in the San Juans, beginning with Ellingwood and Hoag's ascent of Lizard Head in 1920, the development of pure rock climbing areas is of fairly recent origin. The following is an overview of several rock climbing areas in the San Juans.

Telluride

Several areas which offer difficult fifth class climbing near Telluride have received extensive development: Ophir Wall, Ames Wall, and Cracked Canyon. All three areas are located near the Ophir Loop, which is eleven miles south of Telluride on Colorado 145.

The main cliff on Ophir Wall is a steep 650-foot face located northeast of Ophir Loop. A variety of Grade III routes ascend the entire wall connecting crack systems and avoiding overhangs.

Several Grade I climbs are located on the west shoulder of Ophir Wall. There are also a large number of Grade I and Grade II climbs on the 200- to 300-foot east buttress to the right of Ophir Wall.

Ames Wall is a 600-foot, north-facing wall located west of Ophir Loop, across the Illium Valley. To reach Ames Wall, leave Colorado 145 west of the Ophir turnoff and head west toward the Illium Valley on a well-maintained gravel road. Take a left at the first junction which leads to the Ames Power Plant and turn left again before the bridge leading to Lake Fork Junction, where you continue south until the road is blocked off. From there, it is necessary to cross the river before hiking to the base of Ames Wall. Because of the problem with crossing the river in early spring and since the wall is north facing, climbing is most enjoyable in midsummer and early fall. There are several Grade III routes on Ames Wall.

Cracked Canyon is located just east of the east buttress on Ophir Wall. Cracked Canyon contains a large number of 75- to 300-foot climbs. Climbs on the left (west) canyon wall are generally more difficult as they range from 5.7 to 5.12. Climbs on the right (east) side of the wall are generally easier, and there are many easy and moderate fifth class routes.

A guidebook titled *Telluride Rock: An Interim Guide* was written in 1978 by Bill Kees. The guide contains route descriptions in all three areas and also locates several bouldering areas. An overview of the area written by John Harlin III was published in the December 1984 issue of *Climbing*. In addition, a short chapter in *Vertigo Games* by Glenn Randall gives an interesting history of the area.

San Luis Valley

A rapidly developing area is the San Luis Valley on the eastern edge of the San Juans. Most of the climbing is located west of U.S. 285 and north of U.S. 160. Climbing in this area is predominantly on rhyolite, which is noted for its abrasiveness. Most of the areas in the San Luis Valley are single pitch cliffs, although there is potential for development of multi-pitch climbs in portions of the valley. The Rock Garden, which is located seventeen miles south of Saguache and then two and

Don Wallace aid climbing Sunlight Spire during the Chicago Mountaineer's 1979 outing in Chicago Basin. *Photo by Pat Armstrong.*

David Kozak climbing For Ever More near Durango, 5.8. *Photo by Melinda Marinaro.*

one-half miles west on the La Garita road, is currently the most developed area and features both face and crack climbs. There are also several areas which afford excellent bouldering, including the Balloon Ranch boulders. The Palisade area west of South Fork on Colorado 149 is a largely undeveloped area which has a great deal of promise for development of quality multi-pitch climbs. A detailed overview of the area, including mileage logs for access, is contained in an article in the February 1985 issue of *Climbing* written by Lew Hoffman.

Durango

There are a variety of technical climbing areas near Durango. The Watch Crystal is a sandstone cliff located on the east side of the valley just north of Durango. Several climbs in the 5.10 to 5.12 range have been established on the Watch Crystal by local climbers.

Just north of the town, near Community Hospital, is X Rock, which is an excellent practice and bouldering area. X Rock is a 100-foot sandstone tower which has a wide range of climbing routes. There is a large eyebolt located on top of the tower which permits top roping with double ropes. The east face of the tower has some relatively easy face climbing. The south face affords either crack climbing on the X for which the rock is named or difficult face and dihedral climbs to either side of the X. The west face has even more difficult routes including some overhang

Antoine Savelli ice climbing near the Camp Bird Mine. *Photo courtesy of Antoine Savelli.*

problems. There is also an excellent bouldering area just north of the trail between the hospital parking lot and X Rock named the Boxcar. *Southwest Rock* by David Kozak gives route descriptions for the Watch Crystal, X Rock, and the other areas near Durango.

The Pope's Nose

The Pope's Nose is a remote crag in the Weminuche Wilderness which can only be reached by a long backpack. Twelve miles up the Pine River Trail you reach the Flint Creek Trail and turn left. After 1.2 miles, you reach the Pope's Nose, which is located north of Pope Creek. There are several Grade IV and V routes on the south face. Each of the routes involves free climbs of at least 5.9 and varying amounts of aid. To date, there has not been a free ascent of the entire face reported. Route descriptions are available in Kozak's *Southwest Rock* and an article by Ken Trout in the November-December 1982 issue of *Summit* entitled "Colorado's Remote Crag."

SAN JUAN BOOKSHELF

Very few guides or histories deal exclusively with the San Juans. As a general rule most devote a section or two to the San Juans while covering Colorado as a whole.

A discussion of climbing guides must begin with the original Colorado guidebook, the *Guide to the Colorado Mountains*, by Robert M. Ormes, which is now in its eighth edition. Given the scope of Ormes' guide, which covers the entire state of Colorado, the guide is sometimes brief in its descriptions. Nevertheless, Ormes' guide retains its value as an essential part of any climber's library. While Ormes can't give detailed descriptions for each of Colorado's peaks, his guide gives one a good idea of what is available and where to find it.

A Climbing Guide to Colorado's Fourteeners by Walter R. Borneman and Lyndon J. Lampert provides the standard approaches and climbing routes for the fourteeners located in the San Juans. In addition, the Borneman and Lampert guide contains an interesting history for each of the fourteeners.

Borneman has also authored a climbing guide to selected peaks under 14,000 feet entitled *Colorado's Other Mountains*, which includes Rio Grande Pyramid and Lone Cone from the San Juans.

Colorado's High Thirteeners by two of Colorado's most prolific climbers, Mike Garratt and Bob Martin, contains descriptions of the easiest approaches and routes to 169 peaks (69 of which are in the San Juans) between the elevations of 14,000 feet and 13,580 feet. The Garratt and Martin guide also lists all of Colorado's summits 13,000 feet and above by elevation, alphabetically and by topographic map.

A couple of hiking and backpacking guides deal exclusively with sections of the San Juans. Dennis Gebhardt's *A Backpacking Guide to the Weminuche Wilderness* contains detailed trail descriptions for the Weminuche Wilderness, which is located in the central and eastern portions of the San Juans. Gebhardt's guide also provides an excellent map of the trails in the Weminuche.

Hiking Trails of Southwestern Colorado by Paul Pixler gives access and route descriptions for many hikes and some of the easier climbs in the San Juans in the Durango, Silverton, and La Plata areas. In addition, Pixler gives route descriptions for the easier fourteeners in the San Juans. Although it covers the entire state, Bob Martin's *Hiking the Highest Passes* contains hiking descriptions to nine passes in the San Juans.

A couple of guides have been devoted entirely to technical climbing in the San Juans. *Telluride Rock* by Bill Kees gives route descriptions for Ames Wall, Ophir Wall, and Cracked Canyon. *Southwest Rock* by David Kozak describes the rock climbing possibilities near Durango and Pagosa. Kozak also has a section on the Pope's Nose in the Weminuche Wilderness.

The only climbing history which deals exclusively with the San Juans is Mike Foster's *Summits to Reach*, which is a thoroughly researched and annotated edition of Franklin Rhoda's report of the Hayden Survey activities during the summer of 1874. Several books have also discussed the climbing history of the San Juans as part of a larger work. William M. Bueler's *Roof of the Rockies* contains the most extensive discussion of the mountaineering history for the San Juans. Although it is generally geared toward rock climbing rather than mountaineering, Bob Godfrey and Dudley Shelton's history of rock climbing in Colorado, *Climb!* contains sections discussing the 1920 ascent of Lizard Head, the San Juan Mountaineers, and the 1947 ascent of Monitor's east face.

San Juan Country by Thomas M. Griffiths, which is an excellent overview of the San Juans from a geographer's point of view, contains a separate chapter on the climbing history in the San Juans and is illustrated by many of Griffiths' photos from his days as a San Juan Mountaineer. *Vertigo Games* by Glenn Randal contains sections on Ophir Wall, Ames Wall, Durango, and ice climbing which provide interesting insights into the current rock and ice climbing scene in the San Juans.

Many articles in mountaineering journals and magazines such as the *American Alpine Journal, Climbing, Summit,* and *Trail and Timberline* have focused on the San Juans. An excellent tool for researching back issues of mountaineering journals and magazines is Joseph D. Kramarsic's amazingly thorough *Bibliography of Colorado Mountain Ascents, 1863-1976.*

BIBLIOGRAPHY

1. Borneman, Walter R. and Lampert, Lyndon J., *A Climbing Guide to Colorado's Fourteeners*, Boulder, Pruett Publishing (1978).
2. Bueler, William M., *Roof of the Rockies: A History of Mountaineering in Colorado*, Boulder, Pruett Publishing (First Edition, 1974).
3. Chapin, Frederick H., "The San Juan Mountains," *Appalachia*, Boston (Vol. 6, December 1890).
4. Cooper, William Skinner, *Mountains*, unpublished manuscript (1971).
5. Ellingwood, Albert L., "First to Climb Lizard Head," *Outing* (Vol. LXXIX, Number 2, November 1921).
6. Griffiths, Thomas M., *San Juan Country*, Boulder, Pruett Publishing (1984).
7. Hart, John L. Jerome, *Fourteen Thousand Feet, A History of the Naming and Early Ascents of the High Colorado Peaks*, Denver, The Colorado Mountain Club (Second Edition, 1931).
8. Lavender, Dwight Garrigues and Long, Carleton Curtis, *The San Juan Mountaineers Climber's Guide to Southwestern Colorado*, unpublished manuscript (1932).
9. Marshall, Lieutenant William L., "Executive and Descriptive Report of Lieutenant William L. Marshall, Corps of Engineers, on the Operations of Party No. 1, Colorado Section, Field Season of 1875." Appendix A to *Annual Report Upon the Geographical Surveys West of the One Hundredth Meridian, in California, Nevada, Utah, Colorado, Wyoming, New Mexico, Arizona, and Montana*. Washington, Government Printing Office (1876).
10. Rhoda, Franklin, *Summits to Reach*, An Annotated Edition of Franklin Rhoda's "*Report on the Topography of the San Juan Country*," edited and with preface by Mike Foster, Boulder, Pruett Publishing (1984).

11. Ruffner, E.H., *Reconnaissance in the Ute Country*, Washington, Government Printing Office (1874).
12. Percy W. Thomas, "Mountaineering in Southern Colorado," *Alpine Journal* (Vol. XV, August 1891).
13. Woolsey, Elizabeth D., *Off the Beaten Track*, Wilson, Wyoming, Wilson Bench Press (1984).

Magazines and Mountaineering Journals

1. *The American Alpine Journal*, The American Alpine Club, 113 East 90th Street, New York, New York 10128.
2. *Appalachia*, Appalachian Mountain Club, Five Joy Street, Boston, Massachusetts 02108.
3. *The Chicago Mountaineer*, The Chicago Mountaineering Club, P.O. Box 1025, Chicago, Illinois 60609.
4. *Climbing*, P.O. Box E, Aspen, Colorado 81612.
5. *Summit, A Mountaineering Magazine*, P.O. Box 1889, Big Bear Lake, California 92315.
6. *Trail and Timberline*, The Colorado Mountain Club, 2530 West Alameda Avenue, Denver, Colorado 80219.

FIFTY HIGHEST
SAN JUAN PEAKS

Numerous criteria have been devised for establishing what is or is not a peak. A generally accepted criteria is that there must be a 300-foot drop from the summit to the saddle separating the adjoining peak. Other formulas have also required a certain horizontal distance between summits in addition to the vertical drop. The list that follows is rather liberal. I have included all peaks named on USGS maps even if the 300-foot requirement is not met. In addition, I have included all unnamed summits satisfying the 300-foot drop requirement.

As a result, you will find that El Diente, North Eolus, Fuller Peak, and La Garita Benchmark are included although they do not meet the criteria used by others. Although some may accuse me of being too easy, I do not feel guilty. For varying reasons, I feel that each of the peaks listed deserves recognition.

One final word about this list: If you adopt it as a goal, beware of the consequences. You will find yourself climbing some peaks that you are not particularly interested in, to the exclusion of some rewarding climbing.

Peak	Elevation	USGS Quad
1. Uncompahgre Peak	14,309	Uncompahgre
2. Mount Wilson	14,246	Mount Wilson
3. El Diente	14,159	Dolores Peak
4. Mount Sneffels	14.150	Mount Sneffels
5. Mount Eolus	14,083	Columbine Pass
6. Windom Peak	14,082	Columbine Pass
7. Sunlight Peak	14,059	Storm King Peak
8. Handies Peak	14,048	Handies Peak
9. North Eolus	14,039	Storm King Peak
10. Redcloud Peak	14,034	Redcloud Peak

Peak	Elevation	USGS Quad
11. Wilson Peak	14,017	Mount Wilson
12. Wetterhorn Peak	14,015	Wetterhorn Peak
13. San Luis Peak	14,014	Creede
14. Sunshine Peak	14,001	Redcloud
15. Stewart Peak	13,983	Stewart Peak
16. Pigeon Peak	13,972	Snowdon Peak
17. Gladstone Peak	13,913	Mount Wilson
18. Peak 13,895, "Creede Crest"	13,895	Creede
19. Vermillion Peak	13,894	Ophir
20. Vestal Peak	13,864	Storm King Peak
21. Jones Mountain	13,860	Handies
22. Half Peak	13,841	Pole Creek Mountain
23. Turret Peak	13,835	Snowdon Peak
24. Peak 13,832	13,832	Redcloud Peak
25. Jupiter Mountain	13,830	Columbine Pass
26. Jagged Mountain	13,824	Storm King Peak
27. Rio Grande Pyramid	13,821	Rio Grande Pyramid
28. Teakettle Mountain	13,819	Mount Sneffels
29. Peak 13,811	13,811	Redcloud Peak
30. Dallas Peak	13,809	Telluride
31. Niagara Peak	13,807	Handies Peak
32. Peak 13,806 "American Peak"	13,806	Handies Peak
33. Middle Trinity Peak	13,805	Storm King Peak
34. Arrow Peak	13,803	Storm King Peak
35. Organ Mountain	13,799	Creede
36. Peak 13,795	13,795	Redcloud Peak
37. Animas Mountain	13,786	Snowdon Peak
38. Potosi Peak	13,786	Ironton
39. Golden Horn	13,780	Vermillion Peak
40. U.S. Grant Peak	13,767	Ophir
41. West Trinity Peak	13,765	Storm King Peak
42. Fuller Peak	13,761	Ophir
43. San Miguel Peak	13,752	Ophir
44. Storm King Peak	13,752	Storm King Peak
45. East Trinity Peak	13,745	Storm King Peak
46. Grizzly Peak	13,738	Ophir
47. Pilot Knob	13,738	Ophir
48. T O	13,735	Telluride
49. Peak 13,722	13,722	Handies Peak
50. La Garita Benchmark	13,718	Creede

Index

CLIMBERS

Other Outdoor Books from Cordillera Press

COLORADO'S OTHER MOUNTAINS:
A Climbing Guide to Selected Peaks Under 14,000 Feet
Walter R. Borneman
Paperback, 160 Pages, Photographs and Maps

A CLIMBER'S CLIMBER:
On the Trail with Carl Blaurock
Edited by Barbara J. Euser
Foreword by David Lavender
Paperback, 86 Pages, 175 Photographs

SKI TRACKS IN THE ROCKIES:
A Century of Colorado Skiing
Abbott Fay
Paperback, 96 Pages, 95 Photographs

COLORADO'S HIGH THIRTEENERS:
A Climbing & Hiking Guide
Mike Garratt and Bob Martin
Foreword by Walter R. Borneman
Paperback, 250 Pages, Photographs and Charts

ROOF OF THE ROCKIES:
A History of Colorado Mountaineering
William M. Bueler
(New, revised second edition)
Paperback, 264 Pages, 60 Photographs and Maps

For additional information, call or write :

CORDILLERA PRESS, INC.
Post Office Box 3699
Evergreen, Colorado 80439
(303) 670-3010